NYC FROM THE INSIDE

New York City through the Eyes
of the Poets Who Live Here

Collected and edited by

George Wallace

BLUE LIGHT PRESS ❖ 1ST WORLD PUBLISHING

SAN FRANCISCO ❖ FAIRFIELD ❖ DELHI

NYC FROM THE INSIDE:
NYC through the Eyes of the Poets Who Live Here

BLUE LIGHT PRESS
www.bluelightpress.com
bluelightpress@aol.com

BOOK & COVER DESIGN
Melanie Gendron
melaniegendron.com

COVER PHOTOGRAPH
Valery Oisteanu

Interior Collages
"NY Trilogy: Adam and Eve" and "Liberty or Death"
by Steve Dalachinsky

Interior Photograph
by B.A. Van Sise from *"the Infinite Present"*

FIRST EDITION

Library of Congress Cataloging-in-Publication Data

ISBN: 978-1-4218-3717-8

PRAISE FOR NYC FOM THE INSIDE

This is the jungle sung by its songbirds.
  – Kevin Rabas, Emporia Ks, former state poet laureate

A literary accomplishment of skyscraper magnitude.
  – John Burroughs, Cleveland Oh, editor, Crisis Chronicles Press

The pure luminous body of the roaring city I have come to love.
  – Ron Whitehead, Louisville Ky, National Beat Foundation poet laureate

A towering collection, worthy of many days reading and rereading.
  Lori Desrosiers, Northampton Ma, publisher, Naugatuck River Review

Cuts to the heart of its people; a hymn of love to NYC by her greatest inhabitants – her poets.
  – Rab Wilson, Dumfries Sc, Scrivener in Residence, Robert Burns Birthplace

A historic document and milestone in poetry that affirms NYC on the literary landscape.
  – Ian Griffiths, Shotwell UK, Suffolk County Poetry Society

Explores America's iconic city with rugged candor, gentle grace, irony and humor An essential volume.
  – Richard Modiano, Los Angeles, Beyond Baroque

The whole cacophonous symphony which is the city; where the twenty-first century merges with iconic moments from the past.
  – Afric McGlinchy, Cork, Ir, poet and editor

There is an unbreakable bond between people and place, and places gain meaning from their people. The strongest form of this bond emerges between poets and their city. Every city hides life stories deep inside, and those who know how to see, not look, can notice them. And every city has a soul, a heart, a memory, like a poet. To the extent that New York City has become an immortal place, it is in part through the work of its poets.
  – Tozan Alkan, Istanbul Tr, University of Istanbul, poet and translator

Soars to the heights of the skyscrapers in this grand town.
  – Jack Feldstein, NYC NY, Neon Animator

Here we are, NYC's poets, as monuments after the Pandemic.
  – Robert Gibbons, NYC NY, Cave Canem fellow

History, architecture, foodways and poetry of Manhattan and the outer boroughs – The Big Apple – including the downcast and homeless, the community gardeners and mom and pop store owners, baseball, stickball, the Mermaid Parade, parks of all kinds, and the young people who thrive in its chaos.

    – Nancy Solomon, NYC NY, folklorist, architectural historian

New York sounds great and loud through poets' words! New York is a poem that never ends and regenerates itself day after day!

    – Catherine Sorba, Paris Fr, film director

Five stars! A Whitman chorus of poets to give us their love letters to NYC's vivid streets.

    – Cynthia Shor, Huntington NY Executive Director, Walt Whitman Birthplace Association

Just like New York City itself this collection is big, bold and beautiful, bursting with a multitude of voices that reach for the sky demanding to be heard.

    – S.A. Griffin, Los Angeles, actor, author, co-editor Outlaw Bible of American Poetry

The life, heart and soul of New York City...treat it like a bottle of fine wine, from which you pour yourself a glass from time to time and savor the contents.

    – Steve Edington, Lowell Ma, author, Bring Your Own God: The Spirituality of Woody Guthrie

All the excitement of a crowded NYC street, people-watching and realizing you too are one of the people being watched.

    – Denise Duhamel, Miami Fl, FIU, Guggenheim Fellow

Distills and conveys deep endurances in the NYC landscape.

    – Scott Hightower, NYC NY, NYU, Hayden Carruth Prize

Poems that dig the city to its bones! This bold collection bares the soul of the mega city. It is hard to imagine that the chilling reality of underground life beneath New York City's glittering, shiny surface of power can be dug up. But these poems help me understand.

    – Pankhuri Sina, Bihar In, author, poet, translator, critic

New York just like we picture it. A shining testament from voices of truth and love for our world in these dystopian times.

    – Odilia Galván Rodríguez, Placita NM, poet, publisher, activist

NYC FROM THE INSIDE

Contents

INTRODUCTION

When I read the anthology, *NYC FROM THE INSIDE: NYC through the Eyes of the Poets Who Live Here*, prepared by the poet George Wallace, I was reminded of the great poet Walt Whitman and his monumental poetic work, a testimony for eternity. Whitman requires from us – as readers or poets – that we should never stop believing that the words of poetry can indeed change the world, and he advised the readers to never stop dreaming, because dreams lead us to a better and truer world.

This book is written in Whitman's city, New York City, and its subject is that city, seen from the inside and through the eyes of its poets. So of course for anyone who wishes to enjoy New York City, they may embark on such a journey by entering its pages, the best way to get there, and an ideal opportunity to enter this beautiful city through the minds and hearts of those who are in pursuit of its most humane and responsible sound.

But there is something beyond simple enjoyment to be had in this collection – precisely, to hear and to name the beautiful and profound sound that Whitman, in his wisdom, heard in his day; that today's poets continue to hear; and that poets in the future will surely hear tomorrow.

The poems of this book are proof that poets dream and their dreams lead us to truth and humanism, to the beautiful and the sublime. At the same time, they tell us in a beautiful language, of all the disasters of man, the ugliness of life and the awful possibilities of dehumanization.

People in history have always dreamed and will always need to dream. And when it comes to dreams, desires, disappointments, and the enunciation of human spiritual needs, poetry has always been the best way to give those necessary human moments expression.

Life is a desert and an oasis. It is an Eden full of life and liveliness, but it can also be a burned Eden. Life is a dream that lives and one that fades, an innate desire and a gilded one, a day drowning in darkness. And we know that these hidden truths take their best and truest way to the light through poetry. Because art, said the great writer Henry Miller, "teaches nothing, but the meaning of life."

So it is with this anthology, which truly teaches us Miller's simple truth. Especially in turbulent times, when art serves as an ideal opportunity to see beyond the darkness. Especially to the reader of a huge city or in one, who needs to hear the voice of its poets.

Yes, this book is fantastic evidence that poetry is one of the best ways to understand ourselves, the universe around us, and our own feelings, dreams and desires. Poetic dreams expand the boundaries of freedom and imagination, and also educate us not to submit to totalitarian mindsets, formalities, and vanities.

These are the voices of poets living in our time. Their voice becomes the voice of our time, and speaks to and for every reader, in New York and in Rome, in Stockholm and in Pristina, in Buenos Aires and Tirana and Tokyo and Berlin.

– Ndue Ukaj, Prishtina, Kosovo, writer and literature critic
December 2021

About this Book

I

"If only poetry could save us," said nobody ever, until they did – because there are moments in the course of human events when it is only poetry that could save us.

Poetry, written on subway walls. Poetry pinned to the fence around a building reduced by war or conflict to rubble. Poetry shouted out loud or whispered hoarsely inside dim-lit cafes. Poetry enshrined in a cathedral, or pried out of the hands of a junkie and hurled back at the patch of sky from which it came, from the back of a taxi cab or an alleyway behind a local bodega.

The poetry of a great city is no mere anecdote or act of journalistic reportage or political bent; it is neither antidote nor sightseer's tour guide; it is a thing of the city, the city itself, and its voice, constantly on the move, even when it is standing still.

The poetry of a great city permeates the air and peels back the concrete and examines what's hidden underneath. It possesses a fearless attentiveness to the moment, stands at the intersection of what cannot and what must be, and rears its crazy head and laughs.

It is the place where intent and happenstance meet, where human wings take flight or come crashing to the ground. It is what happens at fateful crossroads and out of the way dives; on subway platforms at 3 am and in every corner of every man and woman's heart. It is the place of soul collisions and miraculous escapes; a place for acts of overwhelming courage, kindness, selflessness, or ennui; and yes, for chance encounters; and yes, for transgressions and accommodations and apologies and adjustments and avoidances. And yes, for desperate last stands.

All that and more, materializing, dematerializing, a hundred thousand times a day, in the great eddy and swirl that defines the city and moves within and around its people.

The city ceaselessly under construction, ceaselessly being threatened or affirmed or collapsing of its own weight. The city, reborn 100,000 times a day, both dependent upon and independent of the people who inhabit it, indifferent to their concerns, yet irreducibly fabricated out of the fundamental stuff of their triumphs, their catastrophes and their dreams.

Above all, the poetry of a great city is an act of reconstruction, of prophecy. It is the entire history of humanity ceaselessly revisioning itself out of every possible dream and illusion and actual sad or wonderful experience it contains, no matter how sweeping or small, no matter how it has befallen us.

II

For a couple of hundred years now, the world's great poets, artists and musicians have walked these streets, in good times and in bad. Visitors and transplants from abroad, like Mayakovsky, Auden, Lorca, Breton, Duchamps, Balanchine, PG Wodehouse, Dylan Thomas, Oscar Wilde, John Lennon, Brendan Behan; as it has to American poets born and bred here, or lured here by its promise – Emma Lazarus, Herman Melville, Mark Twain, Edgar Allan Poe, Washington Irving, Henry James, Hart Crane, ee cummings, Djuna Barnes, Edna St Vincent Millay, Arthur Miller, Eugene O'Neill, JD Salinger, Dorothy Parker, Langston Hughes, Countee Cullen, James Weldon Johnson, Paul Laurence Dunbar, Pedro Pietri, Miguel Piñero, Eric Dolphy, Jayne Cortez, William Carlos Williams, Ezra Pound, Louis Zukovsky, Allen Ginsberg, Gregory Corso, John Ashbery, Jimmy Schuyler, Frank O'Hara.

Not only, of course, the poets. Folksingers and filmmakers, and visual artists, and entertainers of every celebrity and stripe – Leonard Cohen, Paul Simon, Joni Mitchell, Bob Dylan, Woody Guthrie, Woody Allen, Martin Scorsese, Frances Ford Coppola, Andy Warhol, Hopper, Mapplethorpe, Jackson Pollock and Jasper Johns, Thomas Hart Benton, Basquiat, Motherwell, Peter Max.

Seinfelds and Larry Davids and Holden Caulfields and Breakfasts at Tiffany. Al Pacinos. Robert DeNiros. Mel Brooks and Broadway Joes. Bowery bums and aesthetes and denizens of the Chelsea Hotel, poor and rich; the tuxedoed best and immigrant taxi drivers who deliver them here or there. All the rhythms, all the metaphors, all the sights and sounds and smells and imaginative expression, all contributing to the Big Mix.

Playwrights and composers and lyricists and jazz pioneers have walked these great streets – Arthur Miller, Eugene O'Neill, Edward Albee, August Wilson, Tennessee Williams, Lin-Manuel Miranda, Leonard Bernstein, Aaron Copland, Steven Sondheim, Moss Hart, Igor Stravinsky, Lois Armstrong, Duke Ellington, Charlie Parker, Miles Davis, Thelonious Monk, John Coltrane.

The world's greats, near greats, forgottens and never knowns, creating timeless art in a timeless city, clapping back at their city, declaring themselves in a strong and unmistakably New York voice. Is it any wonder then, that New York City continues to be at the center and imaginative vortex to many of the key poetic voices in America, if not the world, in 2022?

All the stages for the popular American arts have reinforced the primacy of NYC, from Broadway to Lincoln Center; from Carnegie Hall to CBGBs; from Cindy Campbell's Back-To-School Hip-Hop Jam to the Apollo Theater and Studio 54.

What playwright or novelist, what filmmaker or TV writer, what visual artist or classical composer, wouldn't want to strut their stuff before the greatest stage in the world – Manhattan?

And could all that not spill over into the world of poetry? Ask any poet raised here who, like Lawrence Ferlinghetti, has visited the penny candy store beyond the el and fell in love with unreality. Any poet that came here who, like John Sinclair, chased the ghost of jazz in clubs and on street corners, chasing the challenge of invention with no idea of what might come next beyond the conviction that it would be excellent and funky and fun.

III

And so this anthology, an enunciation of breadth and diversity of voices in 2022 of Whitman's Manhattan. If Herodotus said "you can't step in the same river twice," the pluriverse which is New York City does the old Greek one better – this is a town so vast and contradictory that you can't step into the same river once!

There is no claim to comprehensiveness here – an anthology with any reasonable claim like that would have to be 1000 + pages long – but if you want to know New York City in 2022, ask the poets who have gathered here together in these pages, who give voice to what they know. We think they're a pretty good sample of the breadth and depth of what today's living poets (and those who have recently left us) have to offer.

Ask Charles Bernstein, puzzling out the alphabet soup of subway service changes. Ask Yusef Komunyakaa, seeking green shadows this side of the Bowery.

Ask Gil Fagiani, shooting up with Trotsky. Miguel Algarín, seeking God's garden in the gold and silver flowers of the Loisada. Ask Patricia Spears Jones, admiring three would-be goddesses on the F Train headed for the Mermaid Parade. Or Jeffrey Cyphers Wright, playing matador against the Manhattan traffic, dancing with the horns.

Ask Diane di Prima, hot-plate cooking on Morton St.

Ask Robert Bly who in the muddy shadows of a Sunday afternoon in winter in Greenwich Village sees beaver swimming in a mountain stream, the Missouri River flowing.

Ask Robert Hershon, at Rick's Bottles & Cash, waiting patiently this side of the thick plate glass for his purchase to fall through the chute.

Ask any of the poets of New York in this collection, known, unknown, and incognito, revisiting the old ethnic neighborhoods or cruising the haunted streets of the city side by side with the literary and artistic ghosts of the ever-present tangible past

– adding their own poetic groove and cachet to the tectonic multilayered iconic richness of voice which is the NYC experience, and can leap out and claim you in a New York minute.

IV

Ask the city itself, which is not just a backdrop to millions of stories every day, but a character in its own right, critical to the making.

You only have to namedrop key scenes in the history of American film to recognize that. Locations have agency, NYC locations are often iconic to the fabric of cinematic storytelling. King Kong climbs the Empire State Building. Tony woos Maria at a West Side fire escape. Ratso Rizzo jaywalks on 6th Avenue. Dockworker Terry Malloy raises pigeons on the rooftop of a Brooklyn tenement. Jacob and Jesus Shuttlesworth test their manhood on the basketball courts at Nautilus Playgrounds, Coney Island. Crocodile Dundee fishes from a little boat in the middle of the East River. Tony Manero orders two slices, puts them on top of each other, and eats them while cruising down 86th Street in Bensonhurst.

Two slices or ten thousand, this is New York City in 2022, stacked high and eaten on the run. As ever, it's a rich mosaic, ever-changing, harmonious and chaotic and, as befits Walt Whitman's Manhattan, allowed to contradict itself.

Take your time, stroll through these pages, rub shoulders with Pulitzer Prize winners, legendary movers and shakers, literary outriders and bigshots, and voices in the wilderness, mandated by self-exile.

Each poem is the facet of a gem, and a gem in its own right.

We are the outspoken people in an outspoken time.

Once you truly hear our voices, you'll never be able to unhear us.

– George Wallace
Walt Whitman Birthplace Writer in Residence

Meal Plan NYC, Circa 2000

breakfast:
corner bagel, plain, 50 cents
coffee or hot chocolate
(provided by workplace
on 60th and Park), eat and work

lunch:
one cup fried rice
one egg roll
two dollars
sit in Chinese luncheon or
by Central Park
eat and write

dinner:
small *arroz con frijoles*
y maduros
Café Largo
two dollars
let friends buy you a Corona
eat, read poetry
smoke out front
listen to the Nuyoricans
remember, you aren't
the first to starve with
a pen in your hand

Blues on Avenue C

At night from my window I'd watch the liquor store owner
drag down his metal door, the spray-painted portrait
of his wife materializing above the dates of her birth
& death, she had those eyes that follow
you around, I couldn't see the stars that winter
unless they froze & fell like broken glass, the moon was so
high it looked like an overdose, I was so sick with grief
I wanted to stab a streetlight behind its curtain of fog & deliver
a mournful soliloquy to a trembling little dog under
a blank marquee, the stoplights rocked in
ruthless wind, bicycles churned through the slushy intersection,
a staggering blanket-clad couple paused to argue beneath
the wife's uneven blue eyes, their voices rising up to meet me
full of song & misery

From the Center of the Subway Car

Translated by Pilar González

On my way to work I find fragments of my friend among the
subway drifters
the homeless   the roofless
the beggars
                    the a cappella singers
                    and the schizophrenic.

Some keep their hair in the same unorganized treacherous style
others keep their beards wet   with liquor
there is also one that has his symbolist poet gaze
and his defiant walking style,
        his way of throwing himself to the world everyday like a
knight-errant,
        like Don Quixote but armed with plastic bags
        and disposable cups   stinking of alcohol
                                or dripping coffee.

I continue my trip at the center of the subway car and I watch
them, in silence, my friend has not passed, I repeat to myself
mumbling, like he who
hums a song with headphones on,
he has not died   he has spread out over the world like pollen
and resurrects every day during   my commute among the
subway drifters the
homeless   the roofless
the beggars
                    the a cappella singers
                    and the schizophrenic . . .

Under the Bas Relief of Marx

Under Engels – under pavement he lived –
The eggman – I'd bow to him –
He'd disappear inside a pickly hole
To polish a dozen shells roll
Twine them as we whet our noses
On the diner's brothy beets and bones

An ancient overcoat whistled behind
As I turned to watch a naked thumb slide
A box of lucifers open – invite
Me to peer inside. If not for the guardeye
Of the Bialystoker's zaftig widow
Warming three quivering chins over
Aluminum foil – I feared I'd disappear
Into the garlic folds of the whistler

~

But there below was a shtetl
Looms and shuttles – foaming pickle barrels –
As though etched in copper – crosshatched streets
Formed a tiny square where a lead steeple
Rose to touch the roof of the box
I stared down almost falling into the whistler's pocket –

His skin wattled above me turkey blue
His coat a stübel – a holy man's room
A place to hide his raw and secret lives
A ghetto of gum chewed down to size
Hidden safely in a matchbox
Pulled from the linty silence of a pocket
It frightened me It gave me enormous calm –
His perfect kingdom he placed upon my palm

Amoeba, My City

It's a selfish business, being a city, an amoeba bulging at the
    boundaries,
narrow where orifices lick fulsome tides. It protrudes fat lips to bite
hard scree of the Palisades, chews up Sneden's Landing,
    paints tugs with a
thousand curious villi. What lives in its shifting form accepts
    the island's flux.
Planes come and go, disgorging lives that indifferently cohere.
Women bathe their
children in the shallows before sunning tropical legs.
    An amoeba in a droplet fans
into an island, untidy form. The microscope remarks a secret shell.
In the waste, the sparkling Hudson feeds tugs through the
    locks at Troy,
Collar City; in the body's moist places, it enters and feeds.
    Every death a brief
eternity, a duple split, poisonous through the skin.
    The osmotic city: one.

At Columbus Circle

"If you see something,
say something"
I called to Christopher Columbus,
as he, elevated,
aura-saturated,
hand on his marble hip,
casually overdressed for July,
glanced past frantic cars
zooming in contrary motion
many feet beneath him
while he peered above them
and beyond them
into a dimension

where no one hurries
away from anything
nor speeds toward shifting
fleeting destinations,
because in the afterlife,
the land below, where we are,
is too coarse to pay heed to,
because in the afterlife
the earthly realm
is a whisper scarcely heard,
because in the afterlife
people already are
where they need to be.

Sublime

the world is beautiful
seek it trust it
move towards balance,
yield to its harmony
its peace its pleasure
sublime, sublimity,
above the highest,
on a par with God,
the highest power,
or the self alone
looking for perfection
hold fast
don't hold
open senses to all input,
leave room for fast-forward,
take advantage of roots sown as a child
in this very neighborhood,
in this small island, in this Loisaida,
in this tiny corner of the world,
of the globe, of the planet
plan your entrance
into Heaven,
into God's garden,
into this ghetto of gold and silver flowers,
soon for you'll see
the whole self
not part, but its entirety

Step Four: Moral Inventory

I wouldn't have been able to answer your question anyway, and
so I pretended the car honk was for me, leaned as far over the
balcony railing as I could before thinking of Daniel, then stepped
back, trying not to say *maybe we're supposed to hurt each other* or *of
course I'd like a drink sometimes*, the hard skyline of the city glitzy
in the distance, all the people we've known and fucked and left,
and maybe I'm more like Manhattan than I want to admit: prettier
when lit. It's like when we walked home on different sides of the
same street, and I crouched behind a car to see if you'd notice,
and you didn't, but that really doesn't tell us anything, does it, only
that sometimes you pay more attention to the streetlamps than
to me, and I do the same, like yesterday when I tried to meditate
but kept humming that song instead, and eventually I gave up
and began watching the birds, hundreds of them in formation, a
dark V that swooped and pirouetted against the rose-pink dusk,
and for a moment I finally shut up, prayed only that something
so beautiful would know that it was.

On the Underside of the Brooklyn Bridge

music echoes from jazz alleys
drips from concrete columns
puts the haints on notice / calls them one-by-one
to stand judged / all their transgressions caught
in the dark matter of thirty-second & sixteenth notes

on the underside of the Brooklyn bridge
graffiti collides with the low tones of a bass
washin' the worn down docks clean of their crimes
shadows dancing with ladies of the evenin's
stormy skies as their johns refuse to pay
their pimps refuse to accept the truth

(don't nobody win if the tide don't Argentine Tango with the moon)

on the underside of the Brooklyn bridge
speakeasies' stomp & jive rhythm
hangs heavy in the roadway's steel nets
safety suspended / the ghosts of east & west rivers
praise the passing of melody's golden notes
remove the tarnish from a girl child
found hunched in a dumpster / under-dressed
tryin' to escape the brutal cold
her name unknown / a mystery

(her life pulled from the rivets too frail to hold it)

on the underside of the Brooklyn bridge
the sax plays a ballad for cobble stone
some dimpled by stiletto heels of wanna-be socialites
others brushed & buffed smooth
by minks dragged in after-hour mist
by couples lookin' to remember love
before the jam ended / before the tide rolled out the reality

(their youthful promisin' smiles turned into old everyday excuses
& insatiable yearnings for the dream never caught)

on the underside of the Brooklyn bridge
he is a flash in a warehouse window
shadow dancin' / his arms move from memory
he sees her shimmy a Samba as if wheat in Autumn's breeze
this vision lures him to try again
he hits redial on the phone / holds on until her voice
on the answering machine turns to beeeeeeeeeep...
another sleepless night holds his transgressions / he sighs

(won't she ever forgive me?)

on the underside of that bridge
everyday there is bass & minor scale
sax & major scale / piano & plead / drum & riptide
there is trumpet & fugue / every night
there is an endless lullaby
for the foolish / the damned
the innocent / the guilty

On the Heart of the City and How They Are Disconnected

So this is what you get from your mother,
the belly under the underbelly,
in the off-putting terrain of the heart.
So never get old, dear. Never worsen. And don't
listen to how the ashcans rumble, as you flutter
your eyelashes at the boys. Don't pick up leaflets
about the poor huddling in alleyways on street corners
under stained mattresses or skip to the mayor's office
and ask him to account for the sellout of the city.
But dream instead of decay over a decaf and hang out
at Pret a Manger or Pan au Chocolat. Don't march
in one official door and out the next brandishing
invisible swords and wearing buttons pinned to your shirt
that say RESIST. Never speak of the downside of silence.

Warhol / Race Riot / '63

We were watching the Yankees in black & white on a Magnavox
while across county, or state, there was a billy-club,
a German Shepherd and a white line unraveled on the road.

I remember Hector Lopez' stance, because it gave me a
        spasmodic feel,
like what I would learn later in salsa and mamba,
and even on the screen we could see a white line.

On the other side of the county or state,
black faces were arrested in Liquitex, dissolved by chemicals
so the trace of sweet flowers or burning tires disappeared.

I was watching a relief pitcher named Arroyo, how carefully
        he went
to the rosin bag, how the white powder dusted his hand, and then
I poured a Coke where now there's just pixelating and red wash.

The couch was new leather; the lawns on the block
undulating like outfields into the evening
where the sun flattened in the emulsified sky.

Lightning Streak of White

For Florence Howe, 1929-2020

Black streets, black sky with orchid clouds.
The tide of the day was out. Nothing more
would be carried in – not dreaded, not desired.

Sometimes there was rain, traffic lights streaked on the asphalt.
Sometimes it was spring, all the tiny leaves breaking
out of bud, pleated and tucked. The elevator,
someone with a dog or a bag of takeout, fogged with savory spices.
The doormen who knew me. The taxi. The plane.
The last time, when she begged me to come –
I can't die without you – I couldn't.

Nights I didn't sleep, I'd pour a little scotch.
The deep pleasure, looking out into the dark
and the few lit windows. People
doing people things in their small frames.
Just as I was. Or rather, I wasn't doing anything.
Time released its breath and before the next
there was a little pause. And I lived in that.
Like when you pull the tab on a zipper, the nothingness
between the teeth. She was alive.
Her heavy jewelry hanging in the closet.
Her many pairs of shoes and coats, handbags and umbrellas.

The Alphabet of the Tracks

A's on the F
& D's
the C,
but only
in sector B,
then
runs on N
till becoming
A again.
R's local
on express,
otherwise it's
think Q & G.
L skips
all stops while
O
Terminates
unexpectedly:
take
shuffle bus
if available
or transfer
to V
when possible
.
No
weekend service
on M, T, & E
until June 22, 2023.
Signal problems
on X: expect
delays on the Y & Z.
Late night

service
suspended on every
other line
for an indeterminate
time.

Poem Inspired by Everything

for Charles North

I would just like to point out, but I always end
up pointing in. "Everyone's holier than thou! &
I'm definitely rolling the dice!" a camo-clad
gent w/dark beer a good sixteen fiats away
exclaims – just as I was measuring how to use
inkling in a work: this report brought to you by
the Tompkins Square Park Skocial Mistancing
Fretwork, & Aaron Shurin's elegant purple mask
on Instagram matching a doubled pair of purple
gloves I cycled by on B a minute ago – they did
possess hands, attached to gaily striding arms
accompanied by too-comfortable (a projection)
smiles. My own powdered transparent gloves
make my fingers look dessicated – a thought
parallel to a fuzzy pink gasmask sported by
a fellow strolling by twenty feet away, fifty
masks for seventy bucks at the stationary
store on A, if you ask, grayish blue and intent
a whole other present, my idea of a sentence:
a summary of daily briefings delivered by
rainbow buntings, the horseshoe bar selling
drinks to go to a politely spaced line, & when
the drawn, I mean dawn, distracted from its
game of catch with figure & ground, speaks
I just keep listening to this fish, aghast at
the split fins I and we call legs. I hear sitting
in these fins, sunlight a costume of horizontal
neon bars, early pandemic bloom lines coming
through cracks the clouds briefly perform

Captive

Maybe we all have a bit of Stockholm syndrome
The culture that has kept us captive
Is the one we emulate
Aspire to
Protect
Bleach skin
Straighten hair
Adopt their ideology
Strip dialect from tongues
Made mild of spices
To appeal to their taste buds
Fell in line
Even the ones we think speak change are a tinge too light
The safe kind
The ones that appeal to the masses
Knowing well who "they" are
They're the ones that own your information
Own your freedom
Own your history
That's why many pages left unpublished of an ancestor's
    truth and troubles
Hurts and triumphs
To protect the image of the image we protect
Cycles of protection
Leave room for no reflection
Staring into false mirrors
Of stories altered
From the grace they faltered
See we can be blended as they please
Ripe for the picking
Time after time
We have been walking in straight lines for centuries
Fell in line

To gas chambers
To guillotines
To unemployment lines
To cultural genocide
When a white teen can mock the song
Of an elder
Glimpses of the past made present
Same story
Same players.
See on paper,
My name reeks of rice and beans
Of Boricua beaches
I know what they think upon eyes meeting
Maybe it's because
My skin's the color of the beach floors their ancestors conquered
So familiar to be taken
Tamed
They forget I am an ocean
I am an unruly sea
A world within itself
Roaring
Destined to be free

I know some must be thinking
Yea you're white yourself
Only seeing European ancestors
Like them
Forgetting my name
Forgetting the mixed blood flowing in my hands
Perhaps I'm using this platform
This perceived privilege at best
Just so I can attest
These lines are thin
The thin lines between explorer and native

I guess I'm a testament to just how thin
Just how thin that line is
Between ignorance and embrace
Between the past and future
Between love and hate

Pizza Party

The pizza of today is not the slice
Of my youth. The triangle is small.
The Sicilian is gone. What has
Happened to the slice of my youth?
The sauce is runny. The cheese
Is all oil. The crust is like rubber.
When I was a kid, Forgetaboutit.
When I was a kid, Forgetaboutit.
I guess there is nothing to remember.
It was a different time. Shootings
And drugs and death and AIDS
And welfare and poverty and
The laughter of a child. Hark back
To another time. The train
In the snow during a blizzard.
The cold you dream of in
August. The light strikes
The pond. The pizza slice floats
Away. Oh, to be a pepperoni.
This is where it got tricky.
Stop & Frisk, Frisk and Stop.
Rock and pop. The clip. The lock.
The violence in the park. Where did
All of this hatred start? "All I
Can do is put it in the art." There
Were chalk marks on the ground
And blood stains on the concrete.
Little poor feet running the street.

Three Poems

The Blank Portrait

Dying cities expire slowly.
They cloud, swap industries,
values, for publicity
that is too loud.

Once rambunctious, they
slump, blinkered, top-notch
achievers far too few. Death spins
kitten yarn in a corner of *Alborada*,
a telenovela. Never to step in

too soon, it's foxy. A hundred-
year-old soldier bows in a fishbowl
of bigotry. Oops, what was once a
titmouse is a Rotunda trophy.

The situation is dire.
Death goes to Mexico, drops out.
It can't be speed-dialed.

Plutus

A giant frozen poinsettia is lighting up
Rockefeller Center, a garbled holiday when
atheism is lethal and it is outright treason
to be antithetical. One must join the cub

scouts to arson trees, pump profits from
creekbeds in North Dakota, cage deadheads
from Mexico or, like hysterical women, leave,
ex-pat Sweden with weaned Americans.

The goo is unswallowable. No one can
look at the foxed fable, his ornamental tome
of bromides, his teed-off toxic burn-out

on insulin for a Big Whopper to roil zealots
on a steely crusade. The loneliest janitor can't
sweep dungheap from an unbearable cave.

Fortitude

The end of ambition: how liberating.
Overthinking subsides to incremental
bird-bath robins and other things below
an increasing low ceiling. Urgency, its

status-jockeyed racetracks, lip-syncs
its sorcery upon the young, but how can
that be when everybody is young? It

can. Seven years of basement tax-returns
do not belong to everyone. Trojans on hot
nights turn grey. When you're offered

a seat on the subway, you know it's bad.

Second Avenue

Benedetta Barzini never slept with Gerard Malanga
and she's still furious he faked the whole romance,
all those tender love poems totally bogus
but he looked utterly glamorous
climbing into a cab on Eighth Street
on my third day here in this bulging tent of a city
a real live poet I recognized even if it was
from a Warhol movie it was just like the movie
a movie about the movie everything merged
like day and night merged walking down Second Avenue
past the holy house of Saint Mark's
church of my heart church of the Word
cockeyed spire pointing to fierce American skies
crammed with poets and poems that
filled my head and blended into
the sweet smell of gasoline
the iron roar of Second Avenue traffic
whirling pell mell downtown
a metallic symphony of cars
and cabs and trucks injecting pedestrians
with that click-click speed city rhythm
that urban throb moving your boots
truckloads of food and furniture
shunting and bouncing over the potholes,
Chinese Burmese Indian restaurants
passing in a blur of hieroglyphic neon
Cheap Jack's and *Ratner's* and *Schacht's Smoked Fish,*
and the bodies cooling in the funeral parlor
close by Tony's café deluxe where we
began each day guzzling scrambled eggs
off the formica with the hardcore mulatto ghost ship girls
the chocolate skinned ambulance dancers
I had the fever for their brown eyed handsomeness
but they only loved girls and I wanted

to change that, bevel their edges
reshape their priorities but
they laughed in my face when
I tried to get sexy they were nice
so nice tall dark anacondas
sipping homemade daiquiris
words flying like sparks
as they cracked the dexy whip
left me tongue tied and French fried
dried out drier than Betty Ford;
I let the air outa your sangwich papi…
I tried to emulate their diamond style
with the hot white wire of methedrine
hoping my goofball stare might somehow
shatter hearts when I tottered into bars
on those 8ᵗʰ Street platform heels
doubling my sense of elevation
looking for more than a simple kiss
my arm holding a fist and demanding
a leg to stand on a jambon a whole
Polish ham dripping grease and cracklins
as lunch turned into dinner medulla full of
darts and thorns and dirty deeds
not dreamed but done in moonlight and daylight
doorways and hallways poolrooms and rent parties
broken locks and stand-up cocks
snapshots of a goon world documented
in the flare of a flashbulb
Polaroids fanned like cards in a giddy fist
my faux Borsalino still balanced on my head
as the shutter clicked but the hammer
never came all the way down
and like Sydney Falco 'I love this stinkin' town'
New York the everturning wheel
that grinds exceeding fine.

From Hell's Kitchen: Five Poems

i

They called me Super Baby
I could walk when I was one
They're not sure what I
Have now

ii

I ran women transsexuals heroin
You name it I ran it
I speak 4 languages
Chinese, Korean, Japanese
That's fluently
I wonder what those hormones are
like

iii

I could tell you a story
That'd hush a bodega
darling
But I know you
have to do
Some things by yourself
"Harold that voice so
Strained and sweet
"I'm not going to shake
Hands with you
Because you haven't
Been washing them"
What is it that sets
People apart

iv

I wanted greetings
so bad
Not those, though
You hotel room burning
idiot
from another time
Allowed to exist
through charity
Swaggers nowhere,
Champ
tarry not

v

The old thief
is retired, now
Doesn't know what
to make of life

It's just life, now
Still, I can loiter
Like a pro
We are relieved at this
Brought back

Winter Afternoon in Greenwich Village

It is Sunday afternoon. The shadows seem so frightening
On the brownstone sills. The Missouri River must be flowing
The same muddy brown! The bullboats cross the river
Silently in the naked moonlight. I cannot say
Why a Sunday afternoon in a New York apartment
Should seem to be night among the teepees at Jackson Hole.
Jim Bridger lugs his Shakespeare through the stumps;
In his shack, he swears at Iago far into the night.
Outdoors a beaver swims in the mountain stream,
Feeling with his nose the door of his home like a beehive,
Moving in a darkness the color of Indian hair.
The tips of the small willows move above the silent water.

So Happy to Be Here

beneath my name they've stamped
the city I live in, *new york, new york*
in black ink. The color of permanence.
Am I from here now? Last time I went
home I didn't recognize the place.
Slept outside with the cats and nobody
even offered me a guitar to play. Lately
I've seen so many things worth telling
you. Baby goats with their horns burned
off. An entire living room parked out on
the highway. The clotted evening sky,
the neons of macdougal street, burning
alive. I'm so glad for you; I'm out with
the trash, the warhol dregs and dull-eyed
hippies, the sozzled old punkers and
their new young german wives. I'm
out in the night with your boyhood
friend, he told me your legends once,
how you built an entire car from scratch
just to have a place to sleep. And I'm
hungry for every story, for every neon
light, hungry for the empire state in
blush and blue tonight, hungry for the
vegan place the ethiopian place the
egyptian place, hungry for mamoun's
falafel & the original cappuccino at café
reggio's where I once ate the whole
burning oily plate and was full and
satisfied and alive and here I am now
still alive somehow, listening to every
body's legends and standing on my own
two legs, work-worn, tired, sound awake.

City of Dreams

Stone on stone
we see you, Manhattan
not just as you are now
but as you were,
as you always will be
in our lodges of memory.

Held between rivers
and the deep breath of ocean
you remain the place of many meetings,
words sung in many tongues,
the mother of dreams.

You were never sold,
You cannot be bought.

It's Not so Much His Kiss I Recall as His Voice

A shy pebble rippling water. Each phrase
a school of startled ginger fish shimmering
through the telephone line. I'd like to invite
you to my place & immediately I became
a frightened puppy in a tropical rain forest.
Only to my surprise, I was in Brooklyn
reading Lorca in his living room, calmly
sipping tea. He played me Joni Mitchell
crooning the lines he loved & even tried
to sing the high notes. His falsetto cracking
midair as we both laughed. That's when he
rested a photo album on his lap & pulled
a picture of himself, a young boy swimming
in a Buenos Aires blue reflecting pool. I wanted
to lick the nape of his neck instead said, You'll
have to teach me how to swim. I'm afraid
of water. That's when he placed his lips
to mine, our most perfect palates open as we
pulled away to catch our breath. You have
to be relaxed otherwise you'll drown... I kiss
him again feeling ribs beneath sweatshirt,
our hearts racing the way a diver freefalls
plunging in a sea of pearls

Orange

This is the story
I'm trying not to remember
This is the dream
I don't want to recall
This is the song
of a ball in space

This is the poetics
of nations, religions and cultures
and the way we look to us all

This is the individual
constantly searching for freedom
in a world
Stumblin' thru anarchy and chaos
A cosmos that's
Indifferent to human actions
and the way night turns to day

This is a cacaphonous symphony
of telephonetics and photos
This is the ecstasy of spirits
transparent shapes like shadow
dancing around light

This is a dream
I don't care to recall

This is the carnage that gave us the orange
like the evening that brought us the dawn

Momentary

Timing One
(60th and Lex)

I, running late
cursing stairs
three at a time
because a subway
shredded someone
hit the street
and heard my name
so I spun around
just in time to see
Eddie the Bum
shoot a puke-stream
down plate-glass
fronting patrons
enjoying entrees
and then we talked awhile. . .

Timing Two
(Chambers near Greenwich)

We Was Just Dancing
And Mister That's A Fact
walking the streets
doing Brando
between bars
when a hardhat
suddenly emerged
from an open sewer
pointing and shouting
Coulda Benna Contenda
through a steamcloud
and we was just
dancing with laughter. . .

Timing Three
(Houston at B'way)

what was I doing driving in this storm
my wipers were useless
the streets all blurred
there was rainwater
running through rust-holes in the roof
when I stopped for a red light
a wet arm shoved a laminated sign
against my windshield
one of those guys
that wipes your window down
with a Burger King Bag
my eyes went back to the sign
It read: DUE TO INCLEMENT WEATHER
MY BUSINESS HAS BEEN
TEMPORARILY POSTPONED
perfectly spelled, professional lamination
the man was a giant in his field
I rolled the window down
dug out a five-dollar bill
stuck it between his outstretched fingers
and the rain
kept coming down. . .

The Lovers of the Poor

   arrive. The New York
Times Food critic breathes in rudimentary
outdoor flattops, pats the hand of an old tamale
lady wrapped in a sarape to fend off the
snow. Declares these the real thing.
"Authentic" grilled pineapple al pastor.
Oaxacan mole just like in Corona, Queens where
he arrived
the week before.
                Now they flock.
To "Little México" (his name). Strangle
en español, point to the flags, nod at
the old tamale lady. "This must be it"
they say in fitted jeans, custom blazers
facial fresh, blown bob they nibble on
the edge. Twitter at their travel 40 blocks
to 116th, worry about a cab
clutch
at their purses.
   And they arrive. Starbucks
& Target & Subway. Luxury "towers"
for a community that never goes up
only down.
            So they leave for the Bronx, go
anywhere but "Little México." It's
little Mexico (no accent) now and served
in English with white waiters that say
Tor- Ti- Las as if the Maine toffee & Georgia
caramels they grew up with are still
lodged in their cheeks.
They come now
the lovers of vegan tacos & pilates
& skinny jeaned underemployed guaranteers

they guarantee & arrive show their
visiting parents the tamale lady until
one day she moves to Queens. They
google that tamales were actually made
with pork fat and shrug.

Manhattan

Hot dogs with mustard and sauerkraut
Hysterical women ringing out black luck
Lost on the subway drowning in rats

Who else made a random human hero
Born long ago with obsidian arrow
Victimized by elevators, go straight to hell

Come down the ramp, your father is old
His days will diminish. Manhattan rattles
Rabbi Rabinowitz blooms in Brooklyn

Publish screaming fear, taking advance
It's fair, snow falls on bumpy sidewalk
We do pre-island in plague oh Lord

I have rent control for my faint soul
Upstairs my rooms, it was words made me
Who I am, I am the foot soldier of taxis
If you come inside listen to the avenues
Pay attention to concrete trees, answer
Every kiss, become a question mark

New York New York Bronx is tone deaf,
Lovely late lonesome glass, shoulder
Every exquisite pain of tumbling steel

On the 7

What courage what trust
The weary broken stepped lump
Dropping to sleep on the 4 AM 7 train
Like a hungry haggard unsuccessful Paleolithic
      dude too slow for a successful hunt
No choice but to sleep in a field of flesh eaters
What courage or perhaps how hopelessly
      beat
Do I try and stop the pick pocket
      or mind my own business?
Why are so many scratching their wrists
      and ankles?
I mean snore and scratch scratch
      head nod bounce itch scratch

I looked across the car and I saw an old
      whitehaired working stiff
I felt his sadness, he looked so beat
      so tired
Then I realized it was my reflection
      on the window

What a dangerous city to sleep in
What a dangerous city to weep in
I don't sleep in the subway, I weep
I weep walking the streets
I don't want to call attention to myself
      but my eyes keep leaking
I will not sleep till I throw the bolt
      to the hard wood door
Sleeping with my hatchet reading
You Can't Win by Jack Black

The City

in august 2020 birds got fat
they started turning back into dinosaurs
they didn't miss people
rats on the other hand missed restaurants
the better ones reviewed in the times
there are so many rat snobs
in the infernal month of august 2020
the birds and the rats compete for the future
we humans developed a dream life
that features either wings or fur
in the morning
we shower put on work clothes
and walk into the next room
to work on self-erasure
day and night mean little now
are shaking the jello cube of time
at night me and my friend
jump over walls after putting
phosphorous on our hands
we escape from people
we meet a masked subway rat named Henna
at midnight on the bowery
we discuss astrophysics
sometimes we roll a ball of dark energy
on the rails of an empty train
and then lie down somewhere in the city

Bernie Kletch, Great Downtown Poet

How hard it was to be at your funeral the other day, you who
    always told me death would
be a relief after forty years of marriage. Harder still because
    your wife Estelle carried through
on her long-standing promise to dance on your grave.
    How could she have known the urn would
be so slippery, that she'd go flying off, shoot an aneurysm, and
    join you? Oh, how I miss you
two love birds.

Bernie, I'll never forget the snowy day you Estelle and I were
    walking up 7th when you
took a wild fall off a curb, landing with your legs straight up in
    the air and your head nowhere to
be seen. Estelle and I rushed to your side as soon as we stopped
    laughing, and Estelle had
uploaded a picture of you to YouTube.

In that moment you made the poem that won you the award Poet
Most Likely to Create a Haiku
with His Head Stuck in a Pothole. Here is the haiku:

> Help me I'm drowning
> Pothole is full of water
> Pull me out pronto.

Estelle and I were so moved by those words when they came up
    in little tiny air bubbles
that Estelle said "let's leave him in and see if he comes up with
    another." Eventually, we
did pull you out. And of course you went on to write many
    marvelous poems. All of which
are available in your book entitled *O City, My Head Is In Your
Hole Forever.*

In Search of Giants

I walk at midnight on the Grand Concourse of my mind, trying to achieve the actual location of movie palaces and boulevards. Uphill to the Bronx to the monuments of Woodlawn: obelisks of the Woolworth's tomb and Herman Melville's meek grave topped with rocks and coins for luck. The 4 train ends here a long ways from Arrowhead, with its view of Mount Greylock.

A map of Manhattan that charts only the springs

To point out where the grey spaces turn to hardwood forests and castles. I follow a prayer string from the Battery to the Bronx Zoo, draw myself up by a thread to the fabled worlds above. Find Jim Carroll's lost needles and basketball jersey and shop the covered charms of La Guardia's market on Arthur Avenue.

I never toured Poe's cottage or walked along the aqueduct that brought water from Croton to the city, where he paced back and forth to High Bridge; however, I have driven underneath waiting for his thin body to drop.

Am I afraid?

I've known ravens less voracious and fatter. A locket portrait of his baby wife cracks our windshield. The fallen Poe fastens his coal-lined eyes, fixes a gaze, a bead, to still my heart.

At a forgotten destination
At a damp tomb
I did not climb the wooden and sturdy toothpicks of the staircase. I did not take from the war chest, ribbons and medals or blueprints for a torpedo or smart bomb. Nor did I take quilt blocks nor wooden eggs for darning socks nor board games of checkers or marbles.

Here in this warm space, may obligations fall aside and weep, and my love poem rebound. I want a lover with tree trunk thighs: A young willow that bends with the wind and buds in spring. However, I am cast among the unromantic who powder and spray nature out of our nature and those who hate the feel of moss or dirt.

I dress and prepare to walk a hundred blocks uphill along the Hudson, noting the direction of other people's partners, and the weather and white froth the river sometimes takes on, and the joggers, bikers, strollers, and New Jersey Palisades, those cliffs of amusement parks that once rivaled Coney Island, that island of rabbits.

Or Rat Island
Blackwell's Island
of plague victims

This walk towards boulders of the Northeast, thrusting without sensuality, evading gravity, of pushing the daily upwards, sucking mud through a straw and making bricks. I set my legs to work mixing the muck for a penny a brick.

About John James Audubon, of said Audubon Terrace and Minniesland, take a feather to him.

Walk with purpose and whistle down the avenue
Witness where bodies lie close together
From under the Celtic cross to a ballroom
Homage to fallen bodies of Audubon Avenue

About Birds of America: he had a system. The elephant folio, is not a folio of elephants. Rather Audubon's Elephant folio contains etchings the actual size of North America's birds of prey.

Near a wedding venue, near a trailer park, near the bottoms, near the twin bridges where you can shake off Kentucky mud, near the massacre of Passenger Pigeons, a folio lies under thick plastic, and they turn the page every few days and there is his buckskin suit, his wife's hair combs.

John James Audubon, study these bones
John James Audubon, pay your debts
John James Audubon, set your slaves free

What New York Gave Me

New York City gave me mama in the kitchen early mornings preparing breakfast for us children. Homemade baked Southern biscuits dripping in butter, jam and jelly. Freshly brewed sweet lemon tea and unconditional love. Morning hugs and kisses, running down the street for freshly baked cinnamon raisin buns and buttered rolls. Mama woven stories causing stomach aching laughter. Newly washed and pressed dresses, blouses, skirts, white ankle socks, shiny black polished Mary Jane shoes featuring my reflection when holding them up to the light and reminders to behave in school, even though mama knew they were never needed. Prayers and family hugs and kisses before leaving home. A hardworking mother who sacrificed for her children. Mama going without so her children would have.

New York City gave me a loving and supportive Harlem neighborhood. Caring neighbors. Store owners who looked like me. People I hoped to grow up and one day become. Black children felt safe and loved. The most beautiful and handsome dark complexioned men and women I have ever seen, these images living with me still.

New York City gave me PS 119, a segregated elementary school, beloved Black teachers Mrs. Crosby, Mrs. Edna Rust, Jr. and Mrs. B. Taylor, and our principal, Dr. Eliot Shapiro. All who cared. Affirming and reinforcing in us children America's unsung truth of our beauty, culture and history. Dr. Shapiro's endless pleas for a new school, books and improved conditions, all falling on the uncaring ears of Department of Education officials. Appalled by the failure of Department of Education officials to respond, Dr. Shapiro notified the media. "Here are the horrific conditions my students are forced to meet with daily. Roaches and huge rats scurrying about, gaping ceiling and wall holes, outdated furniture and books ripped and marked in." Handed down symbols of what Black children were worth and expected to be grateful for. As if on cue, our vice principal, broom in hand and students following, chased a huge rat, all caught on camera. Thanks to an outraged principal, teachers, hundreds of parents and a press conference, we finally got our new school. Feelings of love, protection, encouragement and affirmation left with the introduction to Junior High School.

New York City gave me Harriet Beecher Stowe Junior High School 136. Cherished studies, talk of boys, the latest fashions and records. Dreams of romance, holding hands and kisses that never came. Whistles and words from boys draped in youthful bravado. Masking fear, awkwardness and their hidden dreams. Parties and fear of not being asked to dance. Mama's loving words of how beautiful I looked. Word gifts from a mother trying her best to piece together a memory for her child. My prom memories of loving classmates, music and fun. Love replacing tears and a prom dress and patent leather heels two sizes too large.

New York City gave me Evander Childs High School and blatant racism. Glaring hatred when Black students dared to wear our hair natural and African inspired clothing. Remembering Mrs. Veder's kindness and Mr. Henderson who shepherded over our Afro American Club. The blessings of a brilliant student and historian of African History and Culture Noel Irizarry. The courageousness of a group of students who destroyed a racist library mural.

New York City gave me in my late twenties an unhappy unfulfilling marriage. My thirties imagined love relationships, unloved sex and loneliness. My latter thirties and forties wakeup calls and a spiritual and life transformation. A sense of peace. Unapologetically embracing my self-care and learning to love myself first, after years of cutting myself up into pieces, leaving nothing for myself. My fifties and sixties wisdom. A sacred need to accomplish the work I believe I have been called to.

Seventy the age I prayed to meet, brings an abundance of wisdom and gratitude. Seventy and gray hair shouts to me there is no time to waste! The time is now! If not now, when? You have health and an unstoppable thirst and hunger to continue creating and learning. After all, is this not your purpose, our purpose? Are we not here to leave and share what we have created and learned? Are we not here to leave an imprint, not for self-glorification, but to help with connecting humanity past and present?

New York City gave me anger, pain, suffering and sadness intermingled with moments of joy. Dying daily when hearing of another death of a Black man, woman and child. My heart burdened with grief. I try and not mourn the deaths I know will surely come. I worry for the safety of all whom I love and myself. Still, growing out of the ashes of my despair is the struggling seed of buried hope. I pray, call on God and my ancestors and move forward.

Subway Systems

I have a double life the homeless (sha)man said
there are 2 of me
I have 2 selves
I never use them at the same time

I live in double time
I try not to make it a HABIT

N.Y. is my nightmare   my dream
it is what is beneath the tracks
defiled virgin whore
maladjusted transsexual goddess
cross-eyed cross dresser
homeless shaman as greasy as the tracks

I am consumed by jealousy   he says
it is my job to carry this burden
so that you do not

N.Y. is skeleton & frame
heaven hell tributes & lies
the facts as he sees them
skyline & light
city of fallen angels
extinguished stars

N.Y. is nature mort
landscape & EATS
jesus   buddha & god

N.Y. lives on borrowed digital time
like shaman leading a double life
the good   the bad   &   the epi-centre

outside the centre   outside time
a part of & apart from America
what is beneath the tracks
shaman living on outside time

N.Y. is 2 selves
never the same thing twice
never living together
as to not use each other up
body soul
ripped greasy ugly   love
N.Y. is what is beneath the self   the self   the other self...

In an Urban School

The guard picks dead leaves from plants.
The sign over the table reads:
Do not take or *touch* anything on this table!
In the lunchroom the cook picks up in her dishcloth
what she refers to as "a little friend,"
shakes it out,
and puts the dishcloth back on the drain.
The teacher says she needs stronger tranquilizers.
Sweat rises on the bone of her nose,
on the plates of her skull under unpressed hair.
"First graders, put your heads down. I'm taking names
so I can tell your parents
which children do not obey their teacher."
Raheim's father was stabbed last week.
Germaine's mother, a junkie,
was found dead in an empty lot.

Love on the N Train

They're seated on the N train.
Young women snapping gum,
reading dog-eared paperbacks,
love tales, Fifty Shades of Grey,
lookin' for Mr. Right.

Young men, stylin' gold chains, n'
after shave, looking at the girls,
side glances, pausing
at breasts, knees, ankles.

Everyone's looking for love, reading
about love, listening to songs about love.
Even the homeless man slumped across
two corner seats at the end of the car,
dreams about love.

The N stops at Queensboro Plaza.
People with shopping bags and backpacks
rustle on and off. Some run for the doors,
others for newly emptied seats. Books slip
from backpacks, the homeless man sleeps.

A young man sits next to me, music spilling
from ear buds. He moves rhythmically, softly,
keeping time.
His knee brushes mine.

By 57th Street I've danced with everyone
I can ever remember dancing with – at the prom,
strangers at the Fire Island Pines, surviving with Donna
Summers in the disco, the music vibrating in my chest,

the deaf DJ "crankin'em out." Dancing with men,
dancing with women, in small groups and alone.

Then, I remembered the way you held me,
felt your right hand in the small of my back,
your knee leaning into mine. We slow danced
for an eternity, long after the music stopped.

Hot Plate Cooking – 1955

Morton Street – mostly liptons soup at home.   mostly ate
  out at Jim Atkins.   mostly ate english muffins.

Charles Street – more like refrigerator cooking.   hot plate
  not working.   tried to keep milk in the community
  icebox.   millions of red-haired whores and sloe-eyed
  junkies up all night waiting till you slept to steal your
  milk.   once even tried to keep cottage cheese. Left
  in two weeks.

Waverly Place – tim's room and he was bigger than it was.
  could stand in the middle and reach everything in the
  room.   bean soup and very good black coffee.   and
  never to lift a finger, cause you might get something
  moved, out of place, or lost, not to be borne, you
  understand of course.   so you sat on the bed (cot)
  the only clear place in the room, and tim very long
  reached down from shelves different things, and you
  ate them content and waited on in the very hot room
  in the summer.   the hot from the skylight partly
  cut off with a burlap across it.   but still a very hot
  room.   and always with visitors other ones too besides
  you.   and you listened to tales of hitching, mostly
  tall, and of the army, mostly too grim to be lies, and
  home, wherever that was for the shifting people.
  one of them once stayed over, no room on the cot
  for three so he slept on the floor and was long too
  long and his feet stuck out into the hall.

West 16th Street – where susan went to live with her
  lover: beer mostly, and tears, hardly ever both at
  once.

West 20th Street – where I went to live without mine:
    tuna fish lots of it and milk and butter.   an icebox
    that worked.   long room like a giant's coffin, painted
    blue, water bugs and awful curtains no other problem.
    meticulous house.   i mostly ate out, it was summer.

Nueva York

Esta ciudad que acogió mis pasos
y propició el grito desbordado
en mi garganta,
esta ciudad
que me brindó
mesa, pan, amigos,
no me pertenece,
está hecha de sudores ajenos,
de acentos extraños
y palabras vacías.
A veces me envuelve,
me enreda, me atrapa,
otras, me vomita,
y lejos no la extraño
ni la pienso.
Esta ciudad es mi casa.
¿Mi hogar?
Allá, donde el río,
los arroyos y las islas
de la infancia.

New York

This city took me in
and caused this overflowing scream
in my throat,
this city
gave me
a sit at the table, bread, friends,
it does not belong to me,
it is forged by the sweat of others,
of strange accents
and empty words.
Sometimes it engulfs me,

it tangles me, it traps me,
other times, it vomits me,
and from afar I don't miss
or even think about it.
This city is my house.
My home?
Over there, where the river,
the creeks and the islands
of my childhood are.

Fear on 11Th Street and Avenue A, New York City

Now the papers are saying pesticides will kill us
rather than preservatives. I pass the school yard
where the Catholic girls snack. Cheez Doodles and apples.
No parent today knows what to pack in a lunch box
and the plaid little uniforms
hold each girl in: lines in the weave cross
like directions, blurry decisions.
A supervising nun sinks in her wimple. All the things she can't do,
she thinks, to save them, her face growing smaller.
She dodges their basketball.
Who said the Catholic church has you for life
if it had you when you were five? I remember my prayers at odd
     times
and these girls already look afraid.
But it's not just the church. It's America.
I fear the children I know will become missing children,
that I will lose everyone I need to some hideous cancer.
I fear automobiles, all kinds of relationships.
I fear that the IRS will find out the deductions I claimed this year
I made up, that an agent will find a crumpled draft of this poem
even if fear edits this line out... I have no privacy,
no protection, yet I am anonymous. I sometimes think
the sidewalk will swallow me up. So I know when the girls
line up to go inside and one screams to her friend
"If you step on a crack, you'll break your mother's back..."
she means it. She feels all that responsibility, that guilt.
There's only one brown girl who doesn't do what she should.
She's dancing by herself to a song on her Walkman.
One of her red knee socks bunches at her ankle and slips into her
     sneaker.
And the shoulder strap of her jumper has unbuckled so her bib flaps.
Maybe she can save us. I clutch the school yard's chain link fence.
Please, little girl, grow up to be pope or president

The Ballet Called John The Baptist

A man, walking down some street at dusk,
Spies a woman dancing for coins.
He stops to watch from a distance.
The woman struts like a rooster.
She tosses her head back, and howls, like a cat.

He moves closer.
The sun catches the faces of the observers.
Everyone
Is dressed in tatters,
Everyone stoops
As if born in a small room.
The woman steams like a Thanksgiving dinner.
One man beats time with a stick on a junked car.
Another wipes away tears
    with a caked and cynical hand.

They forget everything as the city goes on about its business.
As they circle each other.
Beside himself,
The man leaps into the center of the ring
And begins to dance.
He shakes as if he had just been dipped in a
    cold river
And he laughs; the woman laughs,
The men in the circle laugh.

Until they no longer fit in the world.

New York because I Said so

A day of minutes,
seconds like leaves. Like leaves are disloyal city characters in brittle
congregations. Near shelter dirt and department store cigarette
breaks.

Stale Irish brew,
peels the white away from mid morning eyes that are already
three lies awake. And to make matters worse, our hearts are broken.

Next morning,
our story starts more specific. Hearts don't matter here

Tiled grogginess,
tiling grogginess. A slow flying gutter puddle accompanies a man's
cage walk. Defines his punch line altitude.

This building works hard/This building works the same job for
three generations/This building works as long as epochs produce
money and minstrels/ One third of this building does not know it
is a third/It woke up groggy /We want to get high

Imagine meaningless water
Imagine orphans making a pact to never have kids
Imagine going to work
– this is our first sip

Who knew that concrete would play such a big part in ecological
facts and that mid morning eyes would leak surprise and hate
laughter. Overcrowded is the emotion of conspiracy and toy
property rights

There's only two kinds of people in this world:
One kind owes you money

Category rooftops/Capitalism stands flamboyant/In lines that wrap around water fronts/People pass through/Cadillac swimmers/And children who walk on water/Category rooftops/ That building means margin/Half block toy shelf/Gladiator industry/The Nothing business/The nobody/There's a figure in the window/Why does it always look nervous

The 5 train has pillow cases throughout its Franklin Ave station /
                                    Subway station
                        police remind me of pillow cases

Soundless playground
– this 3am train –

        Childish economics in full self-portrait enthusiasm

In vulnerable slumps,
we race whistling tracks to some cousin of health. This is your
city. Your underground.
        This anonymously high floor became a friend who doesn't
                                            know me
            A writer's mountain where lineage collapses its span into
                                    your girlfriend's cigarette

Also, where strangers lend me temper and proletariat lunch.

Arms between bricks and   midtown fantasy

A manic border
– sort of back then

                        Enemies
                Will not see each other later
                    In america's heaven

New York,
Because I said so

Back to Futurama

Many won't recall this future –
a walk-through millennial fantasy
forecast in Flushing Meadows, Queens
1964, years or decades before
many of your eyes popped open
to former presents, now the past.
But gray legions recall
banner predictions decades back.
The world came visiting, stood
in long lines, rode shiny cars through
product-heaven's promise. Mostly
they revered the stainless steel
skeleton of a world our futures
would flesh out. Orb bold enough
to bridge human divisiveness.

Today no flying cars deliver us
to twenty-five hour work weeks
the humble pencil endures
and there is no Mars colony.
We glide on the hot wind
seat of our pants scorched
phones ringing.
Just pencil the future in.

Three Poems

Mulberry Street

It's the kind of street
that would be behind
one of those crooners
who sang on TV in the 1950s.

A streetlamp, a cemetery
and a big full moon.
What more could a person
want or need?

O to live on nothing
but arugula and espresso,
forever doing penance
in that somber church
across the street.

The one that's surrounded
by a wall that leans on you
as much as you lean on it.

The one full of flickering lights
and statues that talk.
"The dead," they say.
"The dead will outlive us all."

The Courtyard

I call this an ashtray garden
or a handkerchief garden –

really just a small square
spread between two buildings

with a few flowers
embroidered on it.

Not big enough to have a picnic.

Maybe a cigarette
if smoking were permitted
which it isn't.

Muffin of Sunsets

The sky is melting. Me too.
Who hasn't seen it this way?

Pink between the castlework
of buildings.

Pensive syrup
drizzled over clouds.

It is almost catastrophic how heavenly.

A million poets, at least,
have stood in this very spot,
groceries in hand, wondering:

"Can I witness the Rapture
and still make it home in time for dinner?"

The Stoplight at the Corner where Somebody Had to Die

They won't put a stoplight on that corner till somebody dies, my father
would say. *Somebody has to die.* And my mother would always repeat:
Somebody has to die. One morning, I saw a boy from school face down
in the street, there on the corner where somebody had to die. I saw
the blood streaming from his head, turning the black asphalt blacker.
He heard the bells from the ice cream truck and ran across the street,
somebody in the crowd said. *The guy in the car never saw him.*
And somebody in the crowd said: *Yeah. The guy never saw him.*

Later, I saw the boy in my gym class, standing in the corner of the gym.
Maybe he was a ghost, haunting the gym as I would sometimes haunt
the gym, standing in the corner, or maybe he wasn't dead at all. They
never put the stoplight there, at the corner where somebody had to die,
where the guy in the car never saw him, where the boy heard the bells

Shooting Dope with Trotsky

I score some hefty bags of scag
from Old Man Cano on East 118th Street
the *viejito* – 40 plus years in the dope game –
who once OD'd on Christmas Eve
and leaned into a radiator
leaving a burn scar down the middle of his head.

I rush to the East Village
and buy a mess of Trotskyite newspapers:

Vanguard, Fighting Worker, Theory and Practice,
march into a N.Y.U. bathroom
lock myself up in a vast marble stall
and pump Cano's sacks into my arm.

After reading competing accounts
of the 1921 Kronkstadt rebellion,
the Minneapolis Teamster Strike of 1934,
I nod off to the lullaby
of *The ABC of Materialist Dialectics*,
the negation, of the negation, of the negation.

The Pennycandystore beyond the El

The pennycandystore beyond the El
is where i first
        fell in love
              with unreality
Jellybeans glowed in the semi-gloom
of that september afternoon
A cat upon the counter moved among
                the licorice sticks
      and tootsie rolls
   and Oh Boy Gum

Outside the leaves were falling as they died

A wind had blown away the sun

A girl ran in
Her hair was rainy
Her breasts were breathless in the little room

Outside the leaves were falling
        and they cried
           Too soon! too soon!

The Statue of Liberty

All the ships are sailing away without me.
Day after day I hear their horns announcing
To the wage earners at their desks
That it is too late to get aboard.

They steam out of the harbor
With the statue of a French woman waving them good-by
Who used to be excellent to welcome people with
But is better lately for departures.

The French gave her to us as a reminder
Of their slogan and our creed
Which hasn't done much good
Because we have turned a perfectly good wilderness
Into a place nice to visit but not to live in.

Forever a prisoner in the harbor
On her star-shaped island of gray stones
She has turned moldy looking and shapeless
And her bronze drapery stands oddly into the wind.

From this prison-like island
I watch the ships sailing away without me
Disappearing one by one, day after day,
Into the unamerican distance,

And in my belly is one sentence: *Set Freedom Free*,
As the years fasten me into place and attitude,
Hand upraised and face into the wind
That no longer brings tears to my eyes.

The Newer Colossus

My feet have been wilting in this salt-crusted cement
since the French sent me over on a steamer in pieces.
I am The New Colossus, wonder of the modern world,
a woman standing watch at the gate of power.

The first night I stood here, looking out over the Atlantic
like a marooned sailor, plaster fell from my lips parting
and I said, Give me your tired, your poor, like a woman
would say it, full of trembling mercy, while the rats ran
over my sandals and up my stairwell, I was young then
and hopeful.

I didn't know how Europe and Asia, the Middle
East, would keep pushing their wretched through the bay like
a high tide. I am choking on the words I said about
the huddled masses. They huddle on rafts leaving Cuba and we
turn them back. They huddle in sweltering truck backs crossing
the desert and we arrest them. I heard about a container
ship where three Chinese hopefuls died from lack of oxygen
pretending to be dishrags for our dollar stores. How can we not
have room for them? We still have room for golf courses.

I am America's first liar, forget about George Washington.
My hypocrisy makes me want to plant my dead face in the
waves. The ocean reeks of fish and tourism, my optimist heart
corrodes in the salt wind.

Give me your merchandise, I should say.
Give me your coffee beans. Give me your bananas and
avocados, give me your rice. We turn our farmland into strip
malls, give me things to sell at my strip malls. Give me your
"ethnic" cuisine, your cheaply made plastics, give me, by
trembling boatload, your Japanese cars. Give me your oil.

Not so I can light my lamp with it, but to drool it
from the thirsty lips of my lawn mowers. Give me your
jealousy, your yearning to crawl inside my hollow bones
and sleep in my skin made of copper. Look,

over there is New York. Doesn't it glow like the cherry
end of a cigarette? Like a Nebula from the blackness
of space out here in the harbor? Wait with me. Watch it
pulse like a hungry lion until morning. I should tell you to
enjoy it from here. You will never be allowed to come in.

Elevator Down to the 'A' Train

The elevator doors open onto a scene by Bonnard:
photos of babies and cats cover the walls,
a plastic fern and fuchsia hang from the ceiling
and a fake Persian mat is in the corner where the operator
sits on a stool listening to a fugue by Bach.
She pulls the handle to shut the door
and the people become quiet, almost reverent
as they step from photo to photo –
the operator and baby at a birthday party,
the baby holding a calico kitten –
and a few of the riders start to chat:
the resemblance between the operator and baby,
the two of them sitting under an umbrella
that has to be on the west end of Jones Beach
(*and boy was it hot there this weekend*),
an older woman who must be the baby's grandmother.
The subway noise begins to drown out Bach,
the elevator comes to a slow halt and everyone
becomes silent again as they shuffle towards
the operator and hover around the door,
waiting for her to pull the handle the other way.

New York City is a Punk Rocker

Tell your daughter at Port Authority not to look a man between
  the eye
He'll drug her soon into a world of Sugar Daddies, make her
  work the street

Tell her, tell her to keep her eyes looking straight, arch her back,
  walk like a woman
Arch her back, Cosmopolitan, never let a man buy her a drink

Love is a stranger you meet at bars, dark rooms with red bulbs,
  mirror ball
Heart is a dagger, plunged deep into another; lonely women,
  desperate men
Soundtracks of broken hearts to rock and roll, Jamaican bars,
  lead guitars

Liquor pours into the night, cigarette after cigarette, tall tales,
  empty promises
Outside the streets are watching, the air is tall and thin, dry scab
  fingernails
Makeup polish on her face, caked lipstick too hard to kiss but
  you tongue

Inside an apartment you got The Velvet on vinyl, loud stereo
  equipment
In the bedroom you lay her down, she undresses her blouse,
  undoes her bra
Much like other breasts you've seen before, you bring them close
  to your lip

Decking a man for looking at you with malice, breaking head
  with beer bottle

You fight, rolling cigarette rings, the O of your mouth, spread of smoke
She breathes caterpillar breath, look upon her rage; what desire is this

Lydia Lunch in heat, attacking the heart attack, if death should come
    soon
Where will you live not having paid rent, out in the streets, that
heroin hustle
It eats your face, sunk in deep, holes in your hand, long legged,
    muscular

Some nights she straps it on, wicked bang, sounds of uzis in the
    background
Drug dealer at the door, rain on a Monday evening, piss drunk after
hours
Wasting time watching television, listening to Television, the
    Talking Heads

Friends from neighborhood stop by; you roll up blinds; smoke
    them out
Is it someone got murdered or committed suicide, smell of funk
    in the room
Tomorrow, it is band practice; got a gig at the local bar, making a set list

Sister ran away from home, she's come to visit, she needs a place to stay
Got sick of daddy, he liked her pretty; she wants to be a NYC
    punk rocker

So tell her there's a boy on every corner, looking to do damage
Bring her down to her knees, get a tattoo of his name, make
    her draw blood

Tell your mama and daddy, nephews, nieces not to come to
    New York City
She's a punk rocker with tattoos, listens to Johnny Thunders on
    a CD player

Venantius

He was the crazy man
singing the blues between cars
on the A Train –
levitating to the moon
on a painted trail of light.

At the Ringling Brothers Barnum & Bailey Circus,
he released the baby alligators from their cages
during the high wire act,
with lions jumping through feathered hoops
below. Around him, women riding horses
wore pink feathered plumes.
Hawkers sold cotton candy and crackerjacks.

He asked for a photograph
of me playing the cello,
my arm drawing the bow into a long, low note.
I was wearing silk, concert black,
my fingers breathing the music
I played that night.

Around my cello, he drew images
of bears, rivers, waterfalls.
Himalayan peaks,
where elephants, butterflies, fractals
dream in swirling colors
on a mountain trail.

He painted sacred syllables
in Sanskrit, Hebrew, Tibetan
and an ancient Kanji calligraphy –
what he heard inside the music.

After weeks of painting,
he tiptoed over the border
where his *amigos* from Mexico
put his painting in a mailing tube
and sent it to San Francisco.

Inside his meditation, a sanctuary
where the colors swirl and blend.
Outside his window, a river of humanity.
New York City is always a circus.

The Quantum Mechanics of Everyday Life

God doesn't play dice with the world.
  – Albert Einstein

Schrödinger's cat hid out on the Lower East Side,
Incognito genius of quantum mechanics,
Preferring to use his play-dead circus tricks
To nip my mother's calves and brutalize

Mice. Spooked kid, she made the 12-foot dash
From bathroom to bed, barely ahead of that feline's
Canines and leaped – into her nonagenarian's
Scoliotic stoop. From flame to ash

In a blink and a nip. Now, victim or acolyte
Of crazycat, she's always re-running that sprint
From *meydele* to *elter* and back, an event
Cum thought experiment, *mit yiddishkeit.*

God to Einstein: My universe, my bones,
My house, my rules, my ivories, my tombstones.

I am Singing Everything Staten Island

You can see it through the sidelight

Etched in name, etched in deed, *their name was...*

You and me and Staten Island always agree that to disagree is
our dialect

Speed bump, 15 m.p.h., parked car, school basketball hoop empty

Stoops stare back through the empty hallways echo name

Transport the leaving into reflection

Swing the thurible like a chaotic cowboy scattered

Button your shirt and pray to the sea that brought you here

Shoulder bound boat

Connection is who we look into

We are the ferry

We carry us

32 East 64ᵗʰ Street: The Verona

For years, the Queen Bee of the Arts
lived & entertained in this swanky
Italian Renaissance-style cooperative.

Modeled after the Strozzi Palace
in Florence, this gorgeous New York copy
lies smack dab in the Silk Stocking District.

A green canopy flanked by ornate
lampposts – shields Wrought iron doors
opening to a huge lobby

dominated by a winding marble staircase
right out of a Busby Berkeley extravaganza.
Flying past in my yellow taxi

on many harried evenings, I lovingly
envisioned – Kitty Carlisle Hart
descending those rhapsodic stairs

dressed-to-the-nines – to class-up our gritty city.
How hollow my gut feels these last few years
sputtering by in my office-on-wheels

mindful, the gracious lady –
who was emblematic of New York's artsy flair
no longer resides there, but instead –

caped with gossamer wings,
her spirit warbles *Smoke Gets In Your Eyes*
for the radiant angels in Broadway Heaven.

Late Rapturous

Well, the cold iron wind and the Hudson River from whence it
blew, thirteen degrees on all the instruments and water in my
eyes, but there was a fire someplace, it made my ears burn and
sting, and me buffoonish in my old dirty down parka that I used
to sleep in up in the Sierras with my little tent in the snow – I'd
go in on skis by myself and write haiku in the candlelight because
I believed such things would improve my inner being. But now
I was leaning sideways walking up to 54ᵗʰ street to finally have
a look at the de Koonings. I don't know what I expected, I don't
know what I was looking for exactly, except that I'd seen too many
prints, too many cramped photos, and I wanted the full brunt of
it, that late rapturous style, that sexual confrontation that I'd read
so much about, the crazy man in the Fourth Avenue loft before
lofts were ever cool, drinking and working, working, re-working,
wrapping paintings in wet newspaper so he could rub things out
the next day and start over and over and over, yes, it was that, I will
admit it, I wanted to stand in the presence of the real thing and feel
it – it's never the aboutness of anything but the wailing underneath
it, and there was a pain behind my heart and some kind of weird
music inside my ears, so that riding up in the escalators, there came
a slow panic at the swirl of a woman's long skirt, or a man's head
turned at just the right moment – no explaining the sources of
this, not the smells of body heat and heavy coats, though I know
that every time you run toward something you love, you run away
from it too, you get blinded by the colors or you miss something
important and the moment collapses and takes whole worlds
with it, forever, into some kind of blackness. It was crowded,
that room, but almost everybody was just passing through and
I found I could walk right up to those canvasses, and I believe I
could have laid hands on them before anyone jumped me, but of
course I just leaned and stared. I don't know how long. It didn't
matter. What I needed was to take them with me and slant them
against a wall some-place safe and curl up next to them at night

instead of trying to sleep. It would be the only way. Back outside, I staggered up against the wind and it blew my tears back, and I finally ducked into a little place selling hot soup in paper bowls, and everyone was taking something off or putting something on – they were all talking and moving like they knew absolutely how to spend every hour of their lives, and not in darkness, either, or in despair or regret, and when I could see that the winter dusk was running to silver against the high roofs and towers, I stepped out again into the street, the shiny cabs cruising and the men and women bundled in long coats and bright scarves, and the hundreds of windows of the city's dark pavilions each showing its square of yellow light, and I walked back into that other kingdom.

I Want to Marvel at the Universe but All I See Are Bricks

my sister on the west coast and her husband are going to stay in
a tent in Yosemite three days, two nights, they're on the way now

they look forward to seeing Yosemite Falls, a massive 2400 foot
    drop of snow runoff
thundering from a majestic rock cliff to the valley floor below

"It gives off so much energy," my sister says. "Pure energy,
    and the smell of the pine
trees and fresh air. And the sound of the wind rushing through
    the forest."

She worries about mosquitos and bears, apparently there are
more than ever now. She does not worry about the stars, she
looks forward to seeing millions

I check the online webcam view of Yosemite Falls – a six by six
    inch frame
truly majestic. I get distracted by a video of a building getting
    bombed
then turn off the computer and look out onto Bleecker Street

I do not worry about bears or mosquitos
and the stars will live on without me

outside my window I see brick, five stories high, interrupted by
windows reflecting the movement below—streams of people
it's spring in New York City

an orchestra of pedestrians chatter in the warm sun, a radio
    broadcasts

seventies soul, a river of cars and taxis, a siren down Sixth, a man's laugh,
a woman's giggle, I swear I just heard the sound of a young couple's first kiss

and the smell of the bakery below, and cheap perfume, and auto fumes and little dogs
trotting beside two roommates from the apartment around the corner. And there's an
energy here, the energy of people and more people with all their loves and jealousies,
joys and griefs, dreams and nightmares, worried people and people radiating
pure carefree bliss

people that bite like mosquitos and rummage like bears, but mostly stroll on by just
wandering the village as they do on Sundays. A Sunday wander in the city of energy
people like pine trees, the wind rushing through them

the sun will set soon and the night and its energy will bustle forth, neon and a
cadence of high heels and high end sneakers, louder voices and intimate caresses,
the dinner crowd, the bar crowd, the would-be romances coupling home to studios
in Brooklyn or Chelsea, the East Village, uptown and somewhere in the night,
a dwindling to near-silence punctuated by the occasional roar of an Uber or a
late-night lonely drunk

and my sister will see stars in Yosemite
and the stars will live on without me

A Broken Bed and Bodega Beer

Saturday night East Village:
Long "Happy Hour" at Blue & Gold.
Fired up on "well drinks,"
Blondie and Boho
are ready to stalk.

Two coyotes headin' South
prowling the edge of Chinatown
'til they find a joint
with loud music blastin'
from a tenement basement.

Grab a couple drinks
and a seat way in the back
suddenly surrounded
by middle-aged Jersey couples,
fat, tired, and worn out,
lookin' to re-live college days.

Ain't long before Blondie and Boho
are jumpin', swayin',
shakin' hair, and shakin' ass,
bodies vibrating to pounding music,
making out and gropin' between drinks.
Jersey couples stare, awkward and nervous,
embarrassed by this shameless couple,
but secretly wishing
that they still had that passion.

Blonde coyote girl
goin' to the bar for refills
bumps their table
spilling drinks.

Jersey couples are pissed,
They get up and leave;
Don't even wait to see their band.

Just know they're talkin' shit
about the juvenile behavior
of two coyotes around their age
doin' what they're doin'
but I'm thinkin'
they're gonna' go home,
jump in the sack,
and for just a few minutes,
try to be coyotes too.
Good luck with that Jack.

Blondie and Boho stay late,
'til the music's all gone,
head back to the East Village gropin',
thinkin' dirty thoughts,
and itchin' for some "play time."

Those two coyotes
gonna' break that damned bed again,
drink warm Bodega beer,
and hug 'til the sun comes up,
'cause that's what ya' do
early Sunday morning, East Village.

Andrada

I tried to understand the reason
to commune with you, it's rather risky
to compromise the trope on a common
New York statue, if I had a choice

it would be Mnemosyne, the goddess
of memory or Lincoln with his cloak
and cape where the fishbone man
picks dinner from the garbage
to cope

I am where I am
and who is Jose Silva
to bring such a gift, if he is
the patriarch of Brazil
then where is Zumbi

so I sit here in silence
only hear the rhythms of the street sweeper
only Whitman's astronomer in this busy
Bryant park playing ampersand and fellatio
in triple eight

maybe Andrada you can give me
a poem to hide in my pocket
while in quiet reflection
in juxtaposition to Lincoln

with straight coiffure and tuxedo
does not bother me, Andrada
this Ellis Island harbor receives you
and maybe it knows more than
given credit, I rather an Oppen-sky

so I am in repetition, only your
inhibitions Andrada are mine
as singular as isolated, as
ostracized and appropriated

Andrada with your polished patina
and non-compromised demeanor
just keep moving, Andrada
just keep standing, Andrada

there are no blends among the hedges
Andrada, it's tough on a stone bench
looking for a lonely fix
here are only fifteen minutes
this is what I need.

Mid Life Poetry Crises

Sometimes I get sick
of seeing myself
in my poems, my Brooklyn
accent slurring its way
through every line,
whining about settling
into middle age, mostly
on my own, sometimes
lonely, while mulling over
every thing that's missing.

I'm tired of song titles,
retards, autistic kids,
old and new girlfriends,
battered valentines, baseball
metaphors, not getting
laid, subway stations,
working class families,
drunk drivers, dead fathers
and every one else who never
try to talk to each other.

I want to open a window,
walk down a fire escape
without waking anyone,
without leaving a note. Walk
into a bank of coastal fog
and disappear. Come out
on the other side, twenty
years younger, go back
to school, get an MFA.

I want to believe in God,
language poetry, the power
of rhyme. Become witty,
clever and vague, cutting,
but sensitive and politically
correct. Wear a frayed
blazer, shave my balls,
smoke cigarettes, get
an ancient Japanese symbol
tattooed to my bicep, stand
around sipping cocktails.

I want to write poems
filled with abstract meaning,
Greek Goddesses, second
generation immigrants
searching for identity,
down to earth lesbians,
World Trade Center
heroes, villains, victims,
all their greedy relatives.

I want to write a sonnet
about a thin woman
viewing a Matisse print
from thirteen different
angles. Write a haiku,
put a bumblebee in it,
the sound its wings make
brushing a fucking tulip.

I want to open my mail
to submission requests
from the New Yorker
and Poetry. Act humble

when nominations, awards
roll in. Put my agent
on hold. Teach at summer
conferences. Sell more books
than Billy Collins and Jewel
combined. And when I die,
bored, tortured school kids
will be forced to recite
my poems during
National Poetry Month.

Lewis Warsh

You came to the city for all
the wrong reasons remembered
You took the landlord to court
created a no heroin dealer zone
wrote to save the Statue of Liberty
let the kids graffiti their room
turned open arms to newcomers
turned a mimeograph machine on
appeared on public access television
witnessed the ghost of St. Mark's Church
walked from lower Manhattan to Harlem
lived next to glassy park and
won the battle for fair rent

A marriage without proper divorce
Lewis Warsh penned Disorderly Conduct
remembered reasons not remembered
read books to know how to behave
asked intelligent questions
acquired a taste for nameless sinners
accomplished more than some friends
observed long shadows on sidewalks
Was it worth it? Was daily life never enough?
Accusatory thinking and false modesty
accomplished some dignity required to
walk across the Brooklyn Bridge
into higher education

Listening to Coltrane's Olè during the Morning Rush

speeding through the tunnel
with these deep wells / with these
disgruntled / kaleidoscopes
mirror pools / misunderstood
with these   other shards
shake us
shake us
shake us
fly

F train stop for me
let me jump / form a human bridge
let me breathe the air in that car / avoid the eyes of that person
drill the earth

this is the hot excitement
find your train car crush
peripheral vision's gotta be good for something
you know when someone's going to sit on you to make a point
it's more and more common these days

don't push
if pushed . . . don't fall for it
don't fall for it
just listen to John
to Meg & Jack / to Eric
listen to The Raincoats
the wish of the train / the woosh of the rush
the tunnel vision of fluorescents
hurdle through space
get there fast
don't push
just spin the dial
spin the dial
gape in awe

The Good People of New York City

They did not get a good night's sleep,
but woke up to the white
island sun through dirty blinds.

The good people of New York City
sit in a coffee shop, sipping joe
from a chipped ceramic mug
and hum the latest song about
making it in New York City.

Look, there, the good people of New York
still with their tabloids at the corner stand.
They look for a minute like they've forgotten
how to pay, but now look,
they're kibitzing with the vendor
in the red flannel vest.

The good people of New York City
often take the subway this time of day,
but today have decided to walk.
It's only blocks to the copy shop
and already the rain has stopped.

They're wearing tennis shoes
but no sunglasses, since
they don't mind being recognized.

Now the good people of New York
walk through the park
to their favorite stand of linden trees,
where they unwrap knishes
while ducks splash down on the pond.

Look, the good people of New York City
have fallen asleep in the grass.
They dream they are tourists
inside the Statue of Liberty,
but wake up
sure they will never go.

Back at home, our good people
sit on the fire escape and sketch the street.
They'd head to the bodega for a beer,
but it's Sunday. Not that anything's closed.
It's just they need their wits, enough
to talk about the sunset over Jersey.

Then the Chihuahua will need a walk.
Then they'll have to call mother
to let her know that life here is not
what they expected, as good people
of everywhere else.

The Hudson's White Medusa Moon

And now look at the window opening*   of its own accord it opens
And the happy air rises in volume   over the roofs of their street
   Her weightless red roses   sail westward   towards the river
On his back his long blue sleeves float the way the window opens

And the happy air rises in volume   over the roofs of their street
Champagne in their heads   their limbs are lifting   somersaults
On his back his long blue sleeves float the way the window opens
   Where summer comes   a cove of starfish fingers dip in flutes

Champagne in their heads   their limbs are lifting   somersaults
For every kiss   a ruby-eyed pigeon   every cab's a Gershwin song
   Where summer comes   a cove of starfish fingers dip in flutes
Behind the Hudson's white medusa moon   a perfume anemone

For every kiss   a ruby-eyed pigeon   every cab's a Gershwin song
   Sail boats & water nymphs   bell sounds of a simple offering
Behind the Hudson's white medusa moon   a perfume anemone
And now look at the window opening   of its own accord it opens

*Les Fenêtres, Guillaume Apollinaire

Takes on the Bowery

Take 1

Is it an American god or the Egyptian one? What's the difference?
Neither is ever there.

Take 2

We listen to "Funk me up" and go to a hardware store to find a
wrinkled vowel.
We quit happiness.

Take 3

We save a recording of the Star-Sparkled Banner and make
Napoleons for our guests, fix our satellite, wear our baseball caps,
leave the sweep stakes on the counter for later. Don't over think life.

Take 4

My brother listens to Sinatra in the other room as the stock
market crashes.

Take 5

There aren't enough tramps, explorers, and navigators here any
more – only vampire movies. Thank God Anne Waldman and
Bob Holman haven't given up. There's still hope at the Bowery
Poetry Club.

Take 6

My *Islam is Cool* t-shirt pissed you off, but you slept with me
anyways.

Take 7

A foreigner abandoned Jesus last week for a pack of cigarettes
–American Spirits. He named his dog Balzac then Elvis.

Take 8

Time making noise. Yes, we had abbreviated sex—and held on to the prelude.

Take 9

Our faces flooded the water, we argued with the mist, tried to exit a book, to contemplate disappearance.

Take 10

We forget the Arabs gave us algebra. That Thomas Jefferson kept a Koran in his library.

Take 11

Why are all these takes different?

Cause it's New York City asshole.

Blind

The first song I ever wrote was on a bench on Vanderbilt Avenue in Brooklyn on a Sunday when my heart was so shredded, I was bleeding with every exhale, and a man approached me wearing denim around his shoulders and a button announcing his blindness pinned to his chest. I was playing ukulele, singing off-key. He noticed the fragments of valves and veins surrounding me. He told me he loved only once and it was a Sunday NY Times kind of love, when you can't move, all you can do is keep turning the pages, and sink into the research of humanity. He asked me to sing a song about falling in love with a part of me, and I started to cry. He waved his fingers and suddenly they were birds, each one a wing carrying the rest of him closer. He told me he left his sight in Vietnam but that he saw enough to remind him how to remember the shape of things. He said love is orange and hate is wooden planks. He said loss is coral and seaweed and rust. He said that happy is morning, is traffic, is children. I sang him a song about my elbows, the only part of my body I seemed to feel lackadaisical about. He smiled and I could see he left some of his teeth behind too. After he walked away, I wrote a song in my notebook about losing what we forget to notice and then falling in love with what is left behind.

Break Down NYC

Climbing through the bathroom window
skirted with cobwebs, coarse spiders
in tight corsets,
Lost in popsicle orange
vanilla lips, pursed.
Blow me some East River smoke rings.
Let me rappel up your building,
a poet's lurch at skyscrapers.

Las mañanas (yesterdays),
skipping rope in the sunlit
streets of match book
beer can-studded Bed-Stuy tenderized
by the sweltering heat
all along the seashore do that twist
till we reach the Coney Island of Z.
Mind that escapes reverie
I am once again with you.

Strange deafening sounds.
Sirens and silence all in quarantine.
I race – to the top of my building
to do the hustle, wanting to face
large bright stars.
They conjure Tito Puente spirit, Harlem nights
and the rhythms of
Mongo, Santana y always my
girl Billie – at midnight her
bloodshot eyes, writing poems
to still yet Nina and Nikki and Miguel
and the movement that wuz always about
freedom

Hope, a heartbeat, drumming in my aorta
Enlarges my heart,
sugar-caning my veins.

The dreamy past blew in
with their bag of tricks
pieces of the jigsaw cut
from Fifth Ave to Queens, Manhattan,
and the Bronx to Coney Island where my mother's
fried chicken, perfumed by
mango oil, floats in a gust of
white and yellow flowers.

Give us back our memories;
ransacked and extinguished
into shadows – just mix 'em up in
a high ball and walk around
Like a masked time-bomb or a vanishing ghost.
Take your pick, sniff your vaccine
Find *it* again.
Run – begin to bop as the alarm
in your computerized DNA-mind,
synapses firing remind you
that whatever happens next

time is running out.
Mail in your NYC postcards now.

Rick's Liquors

looks like any liquor store
until you get inside and discover
that rick (rick   is that you?)
and all rick's bottles and cash
are behind plastic bullet-proof partitions
and there is no way you can get within two feet
of rick or anything that belongs to rick
we got tired of being ripped off
and locked in the can   says rick
sending your bottle down a little chute

Five Poems

Opening Entrance

She dressed in canvas paintings she got when she divorced her husband,
    a famous post-

abstractionist. I couldn't see her over there in the corner
    at last night's party,

or over on the sofa which lost its geometries at about where her knees
    should have been.

What is it, anyway, with such women who do & don't want to be
    trophies? In any case,

as my friend in his absinthe cups was blabbing about this, her beauty
    abstracted me.

The Philosopher

In New York City in 1939 Ludwig Wittgenstein got his shoes shined
    twice by a lad

Wittgenstein took a shine to, the only American he could say he liked.
    He paid the immigrant

double the usual.... We'll imagine that Ludwig noticed his reflection
    in his shined shoes.

We don't have to know anything else about him.... He's walking,
    his mind is shining,

he has his likes & dislikes, his fears, his paradigms, but it's one foot
    forward with one reflected face,

& then the other, & so on, whole lexicons in his brain shining
in America like his shined shoes.

Time

Andy Warhol's film *Empire*, eight hours of a lens absorbing
& transmitting

that iconic building. That's all, except that a viewer might see
time pass with the light passing;

that's all, except that the light passing is human light passing
in a city passing

through the camera's lens into our own lenses cataracting
a passing building.

Storms

Lady Liberty in New York Harbor passed through a lightning storm
& gained awareness of herself.

Her thoughts became a coppery green patina speckled with
gullshit that made her smile.

She became happier & happier as the days, & then the weeks &
decades, passed by. Immigrants

climbed into her, looked out as though they were her eyes.
She lifted her lamp

up to anyone's god in heaven or wherever. She wept with those
who wept to inhabit her—

she could name them all, knew where they'd come from with
their trunks over-filled with hope....

Then, another lightning storm. She became her inanimate self
again until another lightning storm.

Magnets

In 1945, a boy in Brooklyn, I held onto a horse-drawn ice-wagon,
got running too fast,

fell into the street. That evening, my German mother fingered
my groin. *Ach, du Lieber*!

I remember being in a hospital, my rupture flattened & stitched.
In 2001 my mother told me

that my room would have looked out toward the World Trade
Towers as they burned,

as they fell. That boy propped up in that bed arrives to me often –
he ate ice cream,

healed, played with one black, one white magnet, bombers that
attracted or repelled one another.

Longacre Square

(renamed "Times Square" in 1904)

Whitman, a ferry. Crane, the Bridge.
Seems there is always some hoopla.
In 1901, the area from 37th
to 47th Streets, west side, was home
to a hundred and thirty-two brothels
and at least as many saloons:
Hell's Kitchen, ancestor of the electrified.

Were you ever... pinched in the Astor Bar?
From the carriage trade,
the 1896 Vanderbilt Horse Exchange –
with its shiny brass-trimmed auction arena
and all the horses and their manure
which had to have been dealt with...
to the square as the new home
of the New York Times

and the 1911 Winter Garden Theater
(which still retains – there,
to this day – the shiny brass arena rail):
"Cats," "Mamma Mia," Whatever.

And across the street, some version
of the Taft Hotel: where I – a student
in the 70s... with the likes of Sappho,
Theocritis, or Apollonius of
One-of-the-Far-Provinces –
elected to bus up, attend
Stephen Sondheim's "Follies,"

behold the theater bend back time
and its goat song, an immediate

rebuilding of an Apollonic Loveland!
I vigilantly spied down, across
the street, onto the – (What might it
have been before rehab?) – stage door.

Zoology 19/30

"the circus is in town. The circus is the town, and you never get out of town"
The Original Last Poets

Sundays
the visitors come on tour buses
uptown
double park for blocks
soaking up space and gospel
fill the offering plate
leave before the sermon
don't speak english anyhow
theater of reality is in the street
across 7th avenue at the liquor store
T-bone
does the baboon
pants hanging off his ass
crack cracked out toothless
cameras snap snap
loosey's loosey's he mumbles
got that cheap nicotine
real surreal it all seems
the american dream
can you spare some change
life is a crap shoot
give me a small down payment on the triborough bridge
watch the natives
do the hustle
selling stolen village voices for fifty cent
smile
click, click
next stop sylvia's
now owned by japanese entrepreneurs
to dissuade fear
of a black planet
after all starbucks is

down the street from the apollo
just to make sure
caffeine dreams are realized
the homeless man
with the racoon eyes
opens the door
reaching for a tip
since the stock market dipped
street corner prophets proselytize
screaming about the devil
jesus never called himself a christian
but the holy babble
says god made the devil too
so – boo
we ain't skeered of ghosts
not even holy ones
pour a little liquor for the walking dead
there's nourishment in the cracked plate on the altar by the bodega
owned by Muslims on the corner
just jazz and jibberish spoken here
no jive
don't waste cash on the tour guide book
the djeli speaks in tongues

Eight People

Eight people died
on my block in Brooklyn
last week
and I didn't know
what it meant
to be living
at one remove
from each other,
wary,
isolated,
locked up
with the relentless
bad news
while ambulances
cruised the neighborhood
which was otherwise
so calm and quiet
that I wondered
if God, too,
had gone into hiding
and sheltered in place.

Balaban

I ran down the street and into the house
smelled of oregano and shook Mickey Monaco, said
C'mon, Balaban's got a breadloaf
climbing over old Gruber's fence, he thinks
the mad dogs is doves.

But Mickey grew up in the bed till he was too old
and besides Balaban was crazy, he sucked
his tongue and got left back twice.

So I ran to Joey Bellino's house but his mother's
black stocking said Joey was out early shoe
shining. And besides a, that Balaban he's a
crazy a kid, he suck a the tongue and Joey says
he get lefback three times.

So I banged on Bitsy Beller's window yelled he was
near the top, the mad dogs waiting down
below he thinks is doves.

But when Bitsy stood up he turned into a stiff
cue stick. And didn't want nothing to do
with nobody cracked upstairs.
And Dickie Miller became a semipro. And Howie Fish
a doctor. So I ran down the street full of hope

by myself because I was on fire. But I got there
too late for Balaban. Two of them had a stretch
of skin between their teeth fighting over it,

and the foam of their mouths and Balaban's blood
spattered in such a way, the most the greatest
picture looked me straight in the eye, made me
sit in the gutter and cry,

and when I got up vow to be
Balaban from that day on.

Queens NY, April 18, 2018, 11:17:53 A.M.

There is another world, but it is in this one.
— Paul Eluard

In the moment before touching down
the world-scale reads
zero

the mistake not made
the perfection not yet accomplished

runner   buildings   water

the two worlds
gaze into each other
as if made only by lovers

without form   without text
a single tear
ripples the puddle's reflecting

this moment that cannot be broken

not by the viewer
not by the mortal runner

ignorant   without gravity
hurrying toward a future
suspended
forever for one instant more

let grief and hope pause with her
just above it

as a hand might pause above a page-less notebook
bound in goat skin

(Photograph by B.A. Van Sise, from "the Infinite Present")

Flora Selva

Hidden in my hand
is a rose in bloom
that is my mom.

Flora Selva is her middle name.
Flower of the Jungle.

She took a cutting
of herself
and planted me,
in between
the cracks of concrete
called New York,
where I grew wild and thorny,
a prickly thing
that did not bloom.

A man came by.
He gently pulled me out
and planted me in
the soft cool earth
of a large clay pot
to take me to his Garden State
so I could flourish and bloom.

Hidden in my hand
is a rose in bud,
about to bloom.

That rose is me.

Flor del concreto,
Flower of the concrete.

A Real Stage and Like a Punk Festival or Something Cool and Loud Salsa

Dear Shirley,

This is your first morning in New York and this poem lasts as
long as life
          And the Twin Towers are burning in the sky

and the Chrysler Building is keening and

The Empire State all gray and stolid is etching its shadow
in the neverending breakfast
we call sky

                    Of course all the New York poets are already out
writing poems,
Walt and Frank haven't even gone to bed yet

and we are all feting Elizabeth Bishop who
                    coincidentally
                                        and believe me

          everything
in New York is a coincidence, breathing and walking
                                        even this poem!

                    And your first being here on the very day
(here we

go again!) Senorita Bishop turns
                    like a left turn right into
100 years old,
sing!

So if this poem is long as life and if Elizabeth B. is 100
What does it mean

What does it mean is what we always ask poems
                         but since they are already out ahead of us

they only have time to briefly turn around
                                   in their kickass gym clothing and
           fashion week accessories
                               and shout, Whatever!

                               And tumble on directly and
digitally into a future
where the Poetry Project, Nuyorican and Bowery Poetry Club
               where Poets House, Poetry Society and the
Academy and

Max Fish and all other holy spots like Taylor Mead's bathtub,
Frank O'Hara's haircut
                   and John Giorno's mouth and Anne
Waldman's energy closet

all sit up with Langston Hughes and Allen Ginsberg and Frank
Lima, Julia de Burgos

and rest assured

           (That's the motto of the day, "Rest Assured"!)

                               as your yellow taxi turns the
boogie-woogie criss-cross streets into Mondrian,

           as MOMA becomes Yo Momma, as Harlem beckons
home

And Cai and I will read at the Club at 6pm,
and who knows who will show up

                              Which is the other thing
for sure, that who

will know who, as I know you, as the poem
is now out of sight, and to read it you must catch it

which means you write it

                 like Eileen Myles says
and like Ellison Glenn and Beau Sia say

                              Write it in the sky
                 which is now prepping lunch and your table
is ready

oh so ready
                    to spin

After the Movie

My friend Michael and I are walking home arguing about the movie.
He says that he believes a person can love someone
and still be able to murder that person.

I say, No, that's not love. That's attachment.
Michael says, No, that's love. You can love someone, then come to a day

when you're forced to think "it's him or me"
think "me" and kill him.

I say, Then it's not love anymore.
Michael says, It was love up to then though.

I say, Maybe we mean different things by the same word.
Michael says, Humans are complicated: love can exist even in the
    murderous heart.

I say that what he might mean by love is desire.
Love is not a feeling, I say. And Michael says, Then what is it?

We're walking along West 16th Street – a clear unclouded night –
and I hear my voice
repeating what I used to say to my husband: Love is action, I used
to say
    to him.

Simone Weil says that when you really love you are able to look at
    someone you want to eat and not eat them.

Janis Joplin says, take another little piece of my heart now baby

Meister Eckhardt says that as long as we love images we are doomed to
    live in purgatory.

Michael and I stand on the corner of 6th Avenue saying goodnight.
I can't drink enough of the tangerine spritzer I've just bought –

again and again I bring the cold can to my mouth and suck the stuff from
the hole the flip top made.

What are you doing tomorrow? Michael says.

But what I think he's saying is "You are too strict. You are
    a nun."

Then I think, Do I love Michael enough to allow him to think these things
    of me even if he's not thinking them?

Above Manhattan, the moon wanes, and the sky turns clearer and colder.
Although the days, after the solstice, have started to lengthen,

we both know the winter has only begun.

Outside Ottomanelli's

There was a second there
even though I had forgotten my black and white scarf and the
    April wind
blew the New York wet and cold that can only be blown in New York
when it isn't winter and it isn't spring and the sun hasn't shined since
you got back into town
and there was this still second when I knew spring was coming under
my fur in an animal way like that red sense of food just off awareness
maybe fleet running prey or yellow papaya
but I knew something else some sidewalk satori
all motion ended and focus was tight
and everything CLICKED and I loved New York and I loved
all these people and the deep chocolate taste of grimsweet reality
and felt the spring that I smelt on that absence of breeze
in the middle of the block right there on York Avenue wasn't a matter
of orbits and daylight and axial tilt but rotations and revolvings
of a more metaphorical sort and
rebirth never needs dying
and then I turned into the butcher's and thought about dinner
    (duck I believe)
without even realizing what had just happened and just what it was
that I'd just forgotten.

Ode to Pedro's Unisphere

The People's United Nations
Generously assembled by puntiff
Pedro of the myriad Reyes of punlight
Curated by Larissa with fearless clarity
    at QM
Where all dignitaries photograph cutest

The People's United Nations
Legislature theatre force field analysis
Colloquium speech bubble drone dove
Ocean fertilization seating cube
Tap water chiming weapon-clock

The People's United Nations
Where yesterday's solutions headline
This afternoon's scream:

    "pUN & The U.S. Military
    Re-affirm Massive Haiyan Aid & Relief
    In Spite Of The Philippine Govt.'s
    Rejection Of Bases Re-Opening

    "pUN & Montenegro's Gang Leaders
    Urge Installation Of 24-Hour Public
    Surveillance Cameras In The Black Market"

    "pUN & The President of Somalia
    Call For Re-make Of Captain Phillips
    Feat. Somali Pirates Boarding Ship
    To Hand Out Christmas Gifts"

    "pUN & Azerbaijan's Chief Of Intelligence
    Encourage The Republic's Free Press
    Unlimited Agency Bathroom Access"

"pUN & The Vatican
Stress Joint Initiative To Open
Birth Control Centers &
Abortion Clinics Worldwide"

For only at the People's United Nations
Will urban bush woman dancer moderate
Only at the People's United Nations
Do artists poets activists delegate
Only at the People's United Nations
Is the US of A's face   Joan Jonas

Yeah, *this* People's United Nations!
Rogue summit on nuclear disarmament!
On flowers for Gaia & Garcia Robles!
On the ghost of no más violencia movements!
(Oh the promise of fuller grassWhopper lunches!)

Because let's face it, people—Pedro's
pun will always hold more meanings
(with bees blessing of multiple endings)
than any preamble operative clause resolution
ever called-upon adopted passed by the real UN

For Margaret of Sixth Street

who is probably dead, RIP

Whenever I met Margaret
the rest of the day was magic

Margaret might have been ninety-some,
she never would say. One day

after years of meeting her
on the street

I took the plunge
and kissed her cheek

then watched her grin
around her three
remaining teeth.

Mermaid Parade Poem/June 21, 2014

Three goddesses on the F Train wear red lipstick and carry cell phones
They bestow their boons on those who smiled and waved at them
They smiled and waved back and then they had to get on the F Train
To return to their temples in Carroll Gardens. The red lobster Goddess
Has a slight accent-Slavic. She speaks about a man not a boyfriend,
No "he was my lover" her body shimmers in the coolness of the F
Goddess with flowers in her hair smiles beatifically
as if she knows more than she is willing to say. The crowned Goddess
places her green crown studded with gold sea creatures in front of her,
leaving her head bare,
A loss of Power.
Except, a gold scorpion barrette holds her hair-smart girl.
Goddesses are a dime dozen in New York City, maybe a quarter
a dozen in Brooklyn, where they cast their favors with gusto.
Oh Goddesses who have walked the stairs from the Stillwell Side,
You are now Still and well. Here they are texting on the F Train.
A scented bath awaits each of them. Almond & honey or lavender
Drinks later when the moon hovers and the day
Slowly leaves the bright sunniness to memory and Instagram.

Shipping Out of New York Harbor at 1:25 P.M. on Herman Melville's 200 Birthday

I.E. August 1St 2019

HEAVENS GATE is headed for Whitehall at 16.7 knots
ATLANTIS is headed for NY Harbor at 8.4 knots
OWLS HEAD is headed to New York NY at 22.8 knots
ATLANTIC COMPASS is heading for USNYC at 15.5 knots
SPIRIT OF AMERICA is headed more or less toward
    Staten Island at 16.9 knots
THEN AGAIN is headed nowhere at 4.4 knots
THOMAS JEFFERSON rests at Weehawkin NJ Pier 79
    at 0.2 knots
ANTHEM OF THE SEA heads toward Kings Wharf,
    Bermuda at 0 knots
JEWEL OF THE HARBOR is hiding under the
    Verrazano-Narrows bridge
SPIRIT OF NEW JERSEY is headed to Town Point Park
    at 7 knots
PARADIGM is heading somewhere at 8.3. knots, visible
    from my window
HENRY HUDSON is doing a Harbor Cruise at 4.2 knots
ELANDRA CORELLO AND NANCY P rest near
    Constable Hook
CELESTIAL is heading north at 5.5. knots
MEMORIES MADE lies at 0 knots in Edgewater
DANA ALEXA is headed for Bay Ridge Flats at 1.6 knots
BW RHINE is headed for NL RTM at 0.4 knots
RADIANT PRIDE is headed nowhere at 0.0 knots
DESTINY was traveling at 6.2 knots to an unknown destination
    10 minutes ago

A Kind of Love Story

Walking along Avenue A I was kind of drunk
It was kind of desolate and kind of late
All the stores were kind of closed
And there was this guy who kind of looked like you
He kind of smiled
I kind of smiled too
He kind of waved me over

I kind of went to him whatever
He kind of smoked a cigarette
He kind of put his arm around me
And I kind of let him
We kind of walked over to his place

He kind of had me alone
He kind of showed me his record collection
And we kind of listened to old jazz, the Rolling Stones
He kind of lit a blunt
We kind of smoked it

He kind of had a bottle of Tennessee whiskey
Well, you can guess what we kind of did with that

We kind of kissed in the half shadow moonlight
Then we kind of did other things kind of

In the morning he said he kind of wanted to take me on a long
     car trip
I said I was kind of down with that
I kind of felt I was in love
He said he kind of felt it too

We kind of packed up everything he owned and skipped town
This, because you stood me up
That was very kind of kind of you

A Life Lived in New York City Bookstores

Size Matters (Where It Began)

When I first moved to the Big Apple
I lived in Hell's Kitchen.
I stopped by Gotham Book Mart
and because I was broke
I asked if they were hiring.
"Sure," a manager replied, pointing
to a small table with a typewriter
surrounded by tall stacks of books.
There was a tiny steel chair
almost hidden beneath it.
"If you can fit, you got the job."
I couldn't and didn't. Luckily the Strand,
a much larger store, eventually hired me
so I was able to remain a New Yorker.

It Takes a Pandemic (Where It Ended)

It takes a pandemic
to end a fifty year career of working
in New York City's independent bookstores
which included The Strand, East Side Books, New
Morning, Coliseum Books, St. Mark's and Posman Books
which closed on March 16th, 2020, due to the virus.
The last book I sold there was Camus'
The Plague.

The Last Bohemian of Avenue A (Excerpt)

Joe Top & I decided to give back soil
to itself, following a merry-go-round
in Central Park to harvest horseshit.
We'd lug it here to Alphabet City,
wrap the dung & flower seeds
with cheese cloth, & then toss
the balls into those bare lots
of apartments torched to ashes
by landlords. The sun & rain
began a bidding till the gobs
split open, & wormy tendrils
took hold in the damp dirt –
nasturtium, yarrow, birdsfoot,
cosmos, & rose to kill blight.

I hardly hear early cocks
anymore along my avenue
from C & D, as if trumpets
for the all-night conjurers
& newspaper hawkers
from bygone days. Now,
everything's the next corner
or dust on the fortuneteller's
eyelids. But I can't forget
brazen crowing from coops
hidden among pepper pots,
statues, & birds of paradise.
Those feathered warriors
paraded as if on the edge
of empire or outpost: a cure
for homesickness, fresh eggs
for breakfast, & a little shade
beneath a stunted flame tree.

In a basement room on Fridays
they fleeced dishwashers, janitors,
dog walkers, & short-order cooks.
But Loisaida grew into a refuge
budding towards three rumors
of crepe, green shadows this side
of the Bowery as sweat & blood
sought the brag of Spanish gold.

The Thing About Grids

I was driving for a living, working that night line taxi "tax – ee!"
riding with the rhythms of this wealthy, sleazy city,
bounding up the avenues, trying to make the lights,
Nice piece of driving said a passenger one night,
and they're looking for me everywhere, with
money in their pockets and their hands in the air,
in the corner of my eye, the corner of the street,
the corner of the screen, the windshield I mean.
There's no wind of course – fleet cabs don't have A/C.
But even if there were, you know the coffee's
not always going to keep you sharp,
and it's a matter of life and limb.
And this was the 1980's – traders on the stock exchange
were sniffing lines of cocaine. It was the Reagan Revolution.
And as an independent contractor, I was an entrepreneur!
Hey look at me, I'm filing Schedule C,
and the only one
telling the government
how much I make
is me?
Streams of storefronts scroll by on right and left
traffic in the side streets – like alien craft that are poised to attack.
The roadway is a treadmill disappearing beneath us
and there's not really much of a sky, just gray or black.
Numbers on the street signs count out like a referee
which neighborhood you're into and out of,
your coolness quotient and your chic mystique.
Coke's no good for driving though.
I was more like the bomber pilots in the great world war.
They had their bennies and we had black beauties.
Another cabbie said that's how Elvis got started on drugs,
you know? They gave him speed in the Army.

And I'm speeding up for yellow, with the Don't Walk signs all flashing,
see the cautiously impatient ones stepping gingerly off the curb
and I wonder just how high they'd bounce
if I suddenly jerked the wheel and swerved.
There's a familiar kind of pavement that you'd see all over town –
the blacktop patched-up temporary forever kind
all lumpy with rounded bumps, with metal things protruding,
steel plates and storm drains, manhole covers with steam escaping –
it looks like skin with scabs and stitches.
And it becomes my skin – I see it in my sleepless bed.
I see red and itchy swellings that break open and reveal
structures being pushed out like a veteran's old shrapnel,
miniature versions of the metal in the pavement soup.
And those grates in the sidewalks that
cover the vents for the subway tunnels,
hard, rectangular rigid grids all lined in a row like cars of a train.
I start to see them on the back of my hand,
tattooed over the paths of my veins.
Some professions may be in your blood
but this job is under my skin.
Pull over!
Near a Gray's Papaya somewhere.
And step
Away
from the taxicab.
The city will still be there.

Question Every Thing

so says the poster
in this midtown Manhattan venue
and it has every
and thing
separated
as if they were two different words
which makes it seem like
things are to be questioned
as in the famous quote by
William Carlos Williams:
"No idea but in things"
which would mean going around
questioning tables and tools and
lamps and forks and, well, any
object, but it could mean
the way "thing"
has been used as a substitute for
penis,
which makes me imagine going
around with a microphone asking
penises questions
either literally, like actual dicks
or figuratively, like people who are penises
you know, dicks
but who wants to question
all the dicks in this world?
To what end?
There was a time when I wanted to, and did
question the dicks of the world
either in political debates or
radio interviews (I was what the old
use of the term "d.j." once meant back when
I was 18 in 1960 in upstate New York

and then in the early 'seventies
when I was in my early thirties and was a d.j.
on the first gay radio show, at least in DC)
or rhetorically questioned some of the dicks
in politics or the powers behind the politicians
in speeches I gave when
I was asked to talk at rallies and
protests and demonstrations and
man, I just remembered I used to quote
Karl Marx and say his favorite motto was
"Doubt everything" with the everything one word
in the translation I read
but he might have meant it as two separate words
and been thinking of dicks too.
Marx's favorite motto: question every dick.
I like it.

Bx19

Eagles do not fly
        in New York City,
big mama
            shouts.

So why do I
            have to
go to
        this doctor,

little boy
coughs
        the beginning
                of another winter.

Silver Liner

Swayed by bird song
the May sun reveals
the squalid bones of a city that
hastily pawned its gold

At the light
The bare feet.

By evening untold
silver fish
shine magically on
the receded bank
expired, wilting away
lining the Hudson
with a stench,

all passed,
inexplicably,

by the hundreds.

Low 30s

Luxor
Beauty 35
Like never before
Your eyes
Saw
Say yes
She says
And
Spare me
Hold me,
Spa me
Up the fire
Escape
With all its
Hardware
From the bottom
Of your beauty
Queen
Heart.
Hold and
Spare me
Of the dust,
The wigs
And trust me
Always

Trust me
Always
Tomorrow.

Overgrown Garden: a Love Letter to New York

Dear New York,
I should have left you
when it was easy
could have traipsed
into a spring of sunshine and sparrows
where miles of clean beaches
beautiful sunsets
and the stores
you might take me to
shelved with caviar, Perrier
simple breath
home-baked bread
radiant in light and bright
a costume of white,

still
I allowed you
under my skin –
sweat of summer sidewalks
too much garbage
lingering like an open mouth
spewing a restless mass.
You were gritty
and dirty
feverish
without any relief,

at the corner bodega
you bought me a Slushy
and the voices
of language-
English; Spanish; Arabic; Bengali, Hindi-
a meandering queue

of faces and places
made me dizzy
with desire.

New York
your frantic air is stifling
yet you pull me into this frenzy
of taste and smell and color;
how could I ever leave you?

Even the daffodil
loves to linger
in your overgrown garden.

Kickin' it in 1989

My friend Dimitri decided he needed to quit dope.

He had gotten sucked in, like blood in the dropper. From living
    in the Chelsea.
Hanging with Huncke. New York City in general. Plus, he was
    a guy who was always
ahead of the curve – most addicts then were still smoking crack.

We were going to the Village Halloween Parade, to give him
    something to do instead
of dope. Went by our favorite liquor store on way for a pint of
    Spanish brandy.
It was raining. A Papa Jo Jones working the brushes kind of rain.
A pissing all over
James Dean with the collar of his topcoat turned up in Times
    Square kind of rain.
We needed to be fortified.

But the rain kept away the crowd from the suburbs and Jersey.
That were forcing the
parade to expand its route each year, making it hard to find a spot
    to watch the thing.
This steady drizzle enabled us to amble up to the curb on Sixth
Avenue just before they
turned the corner from 23ʳᵈ Street. Giant puppets operated by a
    bunch of old radicals.
The goths and club kids and breakdancing ghouls. I knew an
    actress who was walking
on stilts, Dimitri had copped with the drag queen Bride of
    Frankenstein. We passed them
our joint, they shared theirs back. When the parade passed, we
    followed it downtown.
Strolling, hands in pockets, like you walk if you belong in New
York City. Watching

the mix of people. The kids. The young ladies. Down to the East
    Village. Cradle of
bohemia. Chillin' with the foot traffic on Saint Mark's Place while
    we drained the last
of the brandy.

Then a drumline keeping time from the direction of Astor Place.
A salsa school marching
their way back from parade's end point in Union Square.
    Timbales hitting rimshots, sticks
stroking the side of the drum, sounding like a skeleton dance.
Bells and whistles stirring
the frenzy as they strode onto Saint Mark's. I looked at Dimitri
    and he said, "Let's go",
and we fell behind them with our dancing shoes on. Other parade
    goers followed
immediately. New Orleans got nothing on our front line. As we
    turned down Second Avenue,
costumed figures stepped back to the curb to give us our turn.
People hung out their windows
to cheer us on.

We had the whole avenue to swing our hips wide. Stamping our
    feet in the potholes down
to the Lower East Side. Up the stairs into the salsa school's
    headquarters, where they
offered us rum with rice and beans, backslapping us like we were
    a bass fiddle's front.

Dimitri didn't use that night, though it would take about twelve
    years for him to kick for
good. But that memorable New York Halloween night got him
    off to a fun start.

The Tiniest Difference

the cars are black
the phones are black
the suitcases are black
the pants are black
the dresses are black
the lingerie is black
the religious clothing is black
the formal clothing is black
it's hard to tell them apart
all the people, wearing all that black
with those black things, in those black things
the people all so similar
their needs identical
their wants all so particular and different
some of them want to punish
some of them want to love
they all need to eat
they all need somewhere to live
the borders are in their minds
their teams, their countries, their religions
the baggage comes down
spit out onto the carousel
traffic in the streets,
goods on the racks, on the shelves
all the people look for theirs
the tiniest difference
a scratch, a stain, a feature, an imperfection
separating it from all the rest

The World Trade Center

I never liked the World Trade Center.
When it went up I talked it down
as did many other New Yorkers.
The twin towers were ugly monoliths
that lacked the details the ornament the character
of the Empire State Building and especially
the Chrysler Building, everyone's favorite,
with its scalloped top, so noble.
The World Trade Center was an example of what was wrong
with American architecture,
and it stayed that way for twenty-five years
until that Friday afternoon in February
when the bomb went off and the buildings became
a great symbol of America, like the Statue
of Liberty at the end of Hitchcock's *Saboteur.*
My whole attitude toward the World Trade Center
changed overnight. I began to like the way
it comes into view as you reach Sixth Avenue
from any side street, the way the tops
of the towers dissolve into white skies
in the east when you cross the Hudson
into the city across the George Washington Bridge.

prior to 1993

Just War

let's bring back crime to the lower east side
bring down those property values
dirty up these brand new windows, break some glass, throw dirt
on these brand new people, make it uncomfortable
for the children of realtors and the trust fund kids the aspiring very
rich with their carefully gelled messy hair and achingly clean blue
jeans with one ripped knee;
organize ourselves into battalions of twelve
sell baking soda out of glassine envelopes, pretend to
nod, put a junkie back on every corner
on every corner stage
gun battles, knife fights; no one has to know
the bullets are blanks and the knives bleed fake blood.
inflatable models of people we used to know
here: put them to sleep
in the night in the park on the benches so the
cops don't know who's who and keep arresting dummies;
we should
all
lie down
on the pavement, pretend to drool, pretend to stink, refuse to move
be whores, walk third avenue, be johns
exchange monopoly money and take each other home
argue loudly, threaten with violence, demand payment on
unpaid debts, put
rage on every corner from union square to east broadway
from broadway to avenue d,
when arrested we'll call it
freedom of expression as an art project guerilla theater, or
just
war

Times Square: the Crossroads

I think of it now as the old city
glimpsed thru cracks
the way an old self sometimes
breaks thru without warning
brought back by those
painted naked ladies buying what
 people want them to sell
pretending they don't; sometimes
I imagine what it would be like
to sneak back there, be one of them
be who I was for a while
disobedient always in trouble who
didn't fit in and didn't pretend to
if I could be that naked-alive again
needs to learn the hard way someone once said...
pushing my way through crowds down streets whose
stores brag name brands and the latest technology,
spot Elmo and the cookie monster
looking like cartoons of outlaws
Columbia university street wannabes
once studied mentored by Herbert Hunke
hitting up a group of tourists
in a cash for photo hustle
something must be done about this
a voice cries out rushing by, and
oh look, there's one of those ladies
heads turning to catch a quick look
fast as it once took to snatch
a gold chain from someone's neck
to take back home with them

The Jazz

for Faruq Z. Bey, at Cornelia Street Cafe NYC '08

The touch is soft
And meaningful
And fast
Like jazz
Uptown
In sweat
In tears
In hard driving notes
That break our opportunities.
High
High
The jazz
The jazz
Can you dig what's happening here?
The blowing future barking
Us back to the dog houses
Of our present lamp,
And the jazz
The jazz
It beats and polishes
Everything
Every damn thing
Let it talk soft
And slow
Let us say no words –
Just listen to the jazz –
To the jazz.

Queens Classics

My Connecticut-bred lover slums in Queens.
To him, Diners are exotic; takes his out-of-town friends
for lumberjack breakfasts they down so fast.

they can hardly catch their breath
to discuss their arteries – or
the sausage links and hash browns clogging them.

For him, Diners are a cultural experience
a dip into the working-class milieu.

I have known Diners forever.
Having grown up in this
brick and mortar province.

The NY Daily News overrates
the Neptune Diner because beefy,
jelly-donut-faced cops from the 114th Precinct
dine daily on too-large-for-their-plates ribs.
Michael's on Broadway has the best rice pudding
– creamy spiked with hard-kernel rice bits.

Astoria's Bel Air attracts the most seniors
because it serves bottomless cups of coffee
on weekends and baskets billowing with mini-muffins.

Pete's Luncheonette, young, sleepy-eyed,
bounce-a-dime-off-my-butt waitresses
know Bayside patrons' orders by heart,
never recite the specials.

They don't look up when my 80-year-old Uncle Matt,
a life-long Queens resident, delivers his lines like Jack Benny:

"…poached eggs, whole-wheat toast without the crusts,
orange juice, decaf coffee…" then whispers behind his hand
"…too many touch the crusts."

Order oatmeal instead? "..tastes like jail food…" says he
who spent one night behind bars for bribing a cop
with four dollars and twenty-three cents …it was all
he and his buddies could scrape together when he was 11 in 1929.

Survival Guide

*– After the New York Times Square sound art installation
by Max Neuhaus at Broadway and 7th*

When the back-to-belly buffing numbs your libido
at the sight of a woman wearing only a guitar
strapped over nipples and crotch
When heat of her "Slow Burn" drowns
in a circus of surround sound
When skyscrapers become a Big Top
alive in digital discord and fireworks of flashing lights
that folds into itself like the theater discount line
And you spin in the merry-go-round of it all
Stumble off and onto Broadway's center sidewalk grid

Stand over the low drone from the subway vent
Let the hum become an Ommmmmm meditation
A drift on the F major monotone
with a kaleidoscope of fall leaves
To the rocking chair of an ocean
The cleansed air from whoosh of waves
A prairie sweet-grass scent after rain
Tune-in to a meadowlark's six-note eulogy
A suck of celebration on a honeycomb
Surrender in the deep South
to the soft hands of cotton in its boll

As the hum becomes a John Cage kind of silence
A Quiet Circus of mindfulness

John Cage: Avant-garde music composer who used silence to enable
ambient surrounding sounds to become the vehicle for zen-like
contemplation

Quiet Circus: A community project along the Delaware River
in Philadelphia that fosters reflective activities of silence,
stillness and placement

If the Spark Whistles

if fireworks only
aim to puncture the atmosphere

if the crackling
splinter flames and scatter

if the spark whistles
or bursts in unannounced

if a triplet staccato clap
breaks silence empty

spills dust on
night-soaked Nostrand Ave,

where Crown Heights braces its walls
in lockdown, summer erupts,

blast and breathless second
give my ears a chance to flinch

questions trail up my throat
and wade behind my teeth,

from living room couch to half-shaded window
I watch myself tiptoe,

too much my grandmother's child
to mind my own

stage a battle crawl on a worn brown rug
devise a shield from an olive-green corduroy chair

hunch shoulders in a coiled bend
taut half-crouch

because I heard
a front door screen lock,
knob lock, deadbolt and
zinc-plated barrel-bolt
latch-slide lock
because a basement door
has two barrel-bolts
because a further door,
only one deadlock
secured with a wood plank

because some nights,
shots clutch my mother's nerves

aimed to puncture
the atmosphere, if only

The Republic

for Frank Serpico

Midnight. For the past three hours
I've raked over Plato's *Republic*
with my students, all of them John
Jay cops, and now some of us
have come to Rooney's to unwind.
Boilermakers. Double shots and triples.
Fitzgerald's still in his undercover
clothes and giveaway white socks, and two
lieutenants--Seluzzi in the sharkskin suit
& D'Ambruzzo in the leather--have just
invited me up to their fancy (and illegal)
digs somewhere up in Harlem, when
this cop begins to tell his story:

how he and his partner trailed
this pusher for six weeks before
they trapped him in a burnt-out
tenement somewhere down in SoHo,
one coming at him up the stairwell,
the other up the fire escape
and through a busted window. But by
the time they've grabbed him
he's standing over an open window
and he's clean. The partner races down
into the courtyard and begins going
through the garbage until he finds
what it is he's after: a white bag
hanging from a junk mimosa like
the Christmas gift it is, and which now
he plants back on the suspect.
Cross-examined by a lawyer who does his best
to rattle them, he and his partner
stick by their story, and the charges stick.

Fitzgerald shrugs. Business as usual.
But the cop goes on. Better to let
the guy go free than under oath
to have to lie like that.
And suddenly you can hear the heavy
suck of air before Seluzzi, who
half an hour before was boasting
about being on the take, staggers
to his feet, outraged at what he's heard,
and insists on taking the bastard
downtown so he can book him.

Which naturally brings to an end
the discussion we've been having,
and soon each of us is heading
for an exit, embarrassed by the awkward
light the cop has thrown on things.
Which makes it clearer now to me why
the State would offer someone like Socrates
a shot of hemlock. And even clearer
why Socrates would want to drink it.

Subway Stairs at Spring Street

Maybe the former factory loft
where I'll be reading poems
is where my mother took me
by the hand up these stairs,
then up a wooden elevator,
to rows of women set to sew,
threading a full day's spool,
where some nice passing lady
stroked her palm over my hair.

Maybe between recited words
machine decibels will purr,
my mother's glance leashing
her child's wayward roam
across a field of tender eyes
flirting with the curious boy
wandered off to see men box
panties like his mother wore.

Maybe from that industrial space
renovated to manufacture art,
at five my mother steered me
around torrential anxious bodies,
countless homebound mothers,
all, she explained, in a rush
to hug their children like me,
waiting in another woman's care.

Maybe I confuse that old address
but not descending these stairs
to ride standing the entire way
back to where windows deceived

in every six-o'clock woman
not the perfection of mother,
real in my hand as she rushed,
coming for me down these stairs.

With Women and Children on the Street

He lifted his shirt
It was a sweaty day
He caught the breeze on his moist skin
    pot belly hairy nipples

No one gasped or pointed
No jaws hung
No one called him "topless"
No one said he was looking for trouble
No mutterings about getting some self-respect
No one violated his space or body
    then blamed *him* for *their* behavior

I fume with envy
Freedom-envy
Freedom to not hide my flab, body hair
    & nipples in shame
Freedom to catch a breeze on a sweltering day

Y'know, all the things that make a woman a "slut"

Key Food

alone at mischance
I wish I were on the ceiling
the guidebook's merry Avenue A
dances with the city's in emotion

a raw stocking of old ground round
who? What? Is the refried beans
Spanish or what the stolen mud cart
across the descriptive clouds on

how'd they erect that bulky steeple
anyway we'll win our victory over
the fucking landlord no refrigerator
she lives in your apartment 30 years

Key Food's selling stolen fucked-up meat
the tenants in this building better organize
what's gefilte fish? It's Jewish?
clouds on knives by crazy ladies

no hand or leg or husband she put her bra
and a box of blueberries in the hallway
on a paper towel with the congressional medal
the purple heart and her t.v. set

you know the sugar for $1.49 is not bad
she waved the biggest knife at herself
dead is the avenue at such expense
the man the corporation lives uptown

he writes a short corporation by heart
part of my washing machine gets mentioned
he pours a long vodka and grapefruit juice
using a young woman of the city as a straw

the roof is leaking and they want you to buy
not only your food but your apartment or else
you've been thrown out millions of dollars
envision the grouchy landlord's ugly asshole

let's plan to make the food so expensive
that the people who live in the neighborhood
will have to move to Sylvania Solid State
to find something cheap enough to eat

Fair for Fare

Today I saw
        a poet
      panhandling poems
    in a subway train,
                    subterranean
                  beneath
                a bustling city
                  of flashing lights
Sandwich-boarded
              between
    a poem
        & advertisement,
                    decrying
                      homelessness
Reading from
    the scribbling prose
                upon a page
            in a composition
                        notebook,
Apologizing
        that celebrity & fame
          are not equated
                  quite the same
            as is fortune & fame;
      Thus, promising
            to *pay it forward*
        whenever life on Earth
                        improves,
He croons
      in perfect Iambic pentameter
                        against
      The roaring railing
                    wheels

against the steel
             of Reality
                  & Life –
Against a will
          Against the wind,
Against the word
            Against the world.

New York at 17

Stepping into the Waldorf Astoria
For the first time feels like
Stepping into the Million Dollar Movie
Breathless I stand staring
At graceful chandeliers
At wine-colored Persian rugs
The finest comforters
Beneath my feet

I am an explorer walking with trepidation
Discovering what is unknown
My mother's daughter
Afraid of doing anything wrong
I enter the powder room
The one bigger than
Our Atlantic City train-row apt
The powder room where
Like Natalie Wood
I recline on a chaise lounge
That stunning cushioned place
Dressed in pinks and mauve
And shiny brass fixtures
That beautiful room
With velvet running water

Lou Reed's New York

In Europe
they're much more receptive
to utility
and famous figures from disco
on skates

In America
if you keep looking for beauty
you'll get run over
by a pylon

to say nothing
of the contradictions
of butcher shops

I believe
we're here at the beginning
of the biggest change ever
and everybody
should be out
making music

I was there
at the beginning
on either side of the vinyl
and I was amazed
at the amount
of wasted
information

Everything was wretched
to say the least

Then God said,
"I'm gonna take film away
but in return
you get three new colors.
We do it with razors
and light animals"

and Michelangelo said
"Wow."

We used to reminisce
about how nice and clean
things were
but now what we miss
is filth.

Talking to the Teeth

(Teeth of enslaved New Yorkers found in
Manhattan's slave cemetery, 18th century)

Now you are one with a skull: its white hush
But sometimes a mouth was a hot leaking
cottage we was all forced to live in

Front tooth, why were you whittled to an enamel fang?
Animal fang? What animal?

Not animal. Enamel. Teeth ingredients. like what you been reduced to: bone
When she giggled. chewed or smiled, some knew
I might be the one thing she clung to from home.

In the children's graves, their teeth were almost always gone
Cause they was the here-born. The start
life. The too-often sugar, corn suppers.

In the back of your mouth, one of you looks like a peg.
Death picks everything clean. Here now,
skinned, buried, lips can no longer
hush us, way a lid might muffle
a pot of cornmeal mush.

And, you, tooth, shaped like an hourglass?
A tooth occasionally tells a skull's time: means I was
born and adorned before this unwelcoming earth.

Night and Day

No sky...
grayness and skyscrapers
tower over me, like robots
about to take my life.
Little windows, their eyes, searching.

What is it about this city that
draws me into it? Maybe it's the
artistic flare, or the way life resurrects
every day.

We sit at The White Horse having beer
thinking of Dylan Thomas.
His ghost gives us the words we need.
Drunk, we stagger home to our shoebox apartment.
We no longer say anything.

Now 5:00AM and the garbage trucks are out,
constant car horns, but I don't hear any noise.
You sleep soundly.
Nearly time to start all over again.

The door to my brick building
has the truth behind it.
The wind rattles windows.
I leave, flag down a yellow cab,
sunbeams –
dart all over the roads,
around buildings, through alleyways and down avenues.

A city spinning, waking me up,
daily with its hum.

New York is Anything

new york is anything
a series of altars
sullivan street tea shop
dawn
bleecker + bowery
samos crack'd 'lectronics
tweed jackets
ghost town
no wave
im solo
communion
crosby + prince

When Our Ancestors Ate Each Other, and They Did

The tour bus is full today, rolling down 7th Avenue
In sunlight so strong it makes one suspicious of everything.
And everything poses for the tourist taking pictures,
Taking videos
     the buildings pose, the parks,
     the Washington Arch
         all the sights in Greenwich Village
         pull their stomachs in and stand straight

And we who are New Yorkers strut down the street
Knowing the other side of everything
And still walking   still strutting

Left foot forward, right arm back
Right foot forward, left arm back

This is the way we walk through life

Listen, the tour guide is explaining everything
And he's got it all wrong.

A Poem

It's a new year; you try to stick your keys in
the door. A neighbor's feet are coming down –
your fingers slip. His wrist goes for
the knob – because he's "in." That's the problem
with doors. The people inside have no patience
with my fumbling. What kind of year is this?
Life is a vow that frightens as it deepens.
You know which ones. I've never written a poem
to you before. Wearing my organs outside.
Or am I in? Lifting myself like a chalice to time.
A can of coke spinning on the floor.
You're right. I'm different. That might be all
we invented this year. In light of the mass
interpretations, translations, migrations . . .
in spite of all that it's great that we did
one single thing – to be different.
And now that it shows we should go really slow.
Wearing our difference like streamers or leaves
bringing our gifts to the city. To watch the
monster unwrap us. Naked and forlorn.
And I'm not like anyone else. Feeling my
foot I hear music. Bridging the city.
It's not the poor, it's not the rich, it's us.
And improved public transportation. And cable TV.
I'm giving up the idea of writing a great poem.
I hate this shitty little place. And a dog takes
a bite of the night. We realize the city was
sold in 1978. But we were asleep. We woke
and the victors were all around us, criticizing
our pull-chain lights. And we began to pray.
Oh God, take care of this city. And take care
of me. Cigarettes and coffee were always enough
in my youth. Now when I wake up thousands

of times in the day. I was in the process
of buying my love a shepherd's flute. And a thin
hand picked the one wanted off the top of the
pile. The one I heard which played so sweet.
And I bought a dud. Hardly better than
a soda bottle. Swell, you said. Well the back-pack
you gave me has started to rip. And the scarf,
well I love the scarf but I keep re-living
that Canal Jean remark. Cause there's no place
for the ironic in plain living. It goes too
fast so you must be direct. Symbolically
I want my black jersey back. Realistically
you must give it to me because I will keep
talking to your machine if you don't.
Our mayor is a murderer, our president
is a killer, Jean Harris is still not
free which leads me to question the
ethics of our governor who I thought
was good. There is an argument
for poetry being deep but I am not that argument.
There is an argument which chiefly has to do
with judging things which have nothing
to do with money as worthless
because you don't make any money from them.
Did you call your mother a fool when
she gave you your oatmeal in the morning.
I cannot explain my life from the point of
view of all the nooks and crannies
I occupied in my childhood yet
there I sat, smoking. More than anything
I want privacy. If I keep doing this
you will leave me alone. And what about
poor children. Dying in the street
in Calcutta today. Or little swollen
bellies in Africa. A public death

of course has no song. At some point
I decided I would want to die
in my home. And so I would have
to have it, as others would
have to have none. Sometime
after they sold New York
I began seeing you. I was dreaming
but I felt your judgment, and I saw
your face. And a woman stepped out of my
house and she opened the door.

We Used to Call Manhattan 'The City' as if Queens Didn't Count

This train is a slow-moving whisper
that curves at an impossible angle.

> This whisper is spoken in
> one hundred and thirty-eight
> different mother tongues at once.

This train may stall but
is a hard-working routine
tinged with promise.

> This promise teeters
> over roads and schoolyards
> and is a city unto itself.

Somewhere below someone
is crossing a threshold. Someone
stands in a small room and
packs a sack of empanadas or
samosas or a foil-wrapped
lunch.

> This train speeds past the mosque
> and the Korean church that was
> once a Jewish temple. Its cars
> rattle above the night market and
> the South Asian sweet shop.

A child rises in a small room
then boards this train
carrying an enormous thought
that curves at an equally

impossible angle. It teeters
around the bend but
does not fall.

>   She eavesdrops on two point
>   three million moments tinged
>   with challenge or promise.
>   Each moment curves at an
>   impossible angle before
>   entering the world at large.

Some of these moments are
spoken in any one of one hundred
and thirty-eight different home
languages. They are a city
unto themselves.

>   This train's passengers
>   eavesdrop on each other's
>   routines or hope-tinged
>   moments. They steal seconds
>   of eye-contact and
>   regard each other
>   in silence.

Three Poems

1. Devotional

The movie fades
to your hands
           on my lower back

because you saw me,
           wanted to see me.

Because you spoke
           of train tracks

on an emptied-out
New York City.

That home that gave us
so much and took
           so much.

There were places
we needed to go.
           Survival was not enough.

Beauty to beauty:
woman and poem and city.

2. While Morning Cracks

An aftermath
that punched you
right in the gut.

A rift on the dust jacket.
A trail past fuckers
in Brownstones.

At the chapel window:
a man in love
with brushstrokes
& a peppery
greatness.

You had lusts to spare.

A place to be
while morning cracks
the seal of geography.

3. This Is Living

This is how we do it
with the car wash attendant
on duty. A world you badly
want to be a part of. This
gives me goosebumps. I can't
stop watching you southing. A
worried man washing his
clothes. Cross the yellow street.
You're tangled with the woman
up the ladder. Walk barefooted
on the pavement. For all the
lights past and ahead. Try imagining
where a broom is not taken
for granted. This is living. We
held each other all night, nothing more.

concourse discourse (off course)

Bronx improvisation, 2015

i think i got   cut off there   but i was saying how   you'll
notice   that where   the glio community garden once stood   or
nearby really   there now stands a community garden   given to
bathgate from the top down   in typical post-bloomberg new york
fashion   where we associate gardens   and greenspace   with
acts of corporate philanthropy   and power-drunk broker crumb-
tossing   rather than acts of resistance and struggle and survival
and sharing and beauty and family and history   the history of
casitas   the history of   opposition to urban renewal and its
top-down policies   surviving to this day   i think i've shown
you   what i wanted to show you   so i'll just walk and bleat
and let myself   be incomplete in meaning   my mumblephonics
my mnemonics of forgetting   my preamble to ambling   as if
i knew how to do anything else   it's the night of the big fight
pacquiao-mayweather   i heard abuelitas even   debating it on
park benches   but i have my own fight   on my hands   i'm
twelve rounds against this phone   its memory of apps and its
happenstance of memory   see the cross bronx again   see the
amparo salvage   amparo   refuge   salvage   what we're all
seeking   what poetry has given me   what i beg of it   new york
public library   my smartphone book   is public i guess   in its
own way   but not library material   look at that house   whom
does it house   look at ps 58   what time is it?   i guess it's
always time for prayer   says garden of prayer cathedral   masjid
ghurabaa ahlul sunnah   tires and wheels   iglesia cristiana   more
rims   more rhymes   change always requires our participation
sewer mechanical or elsewhere   for warding off the corporations
even as we seek our own corporeal logic   what can we express
in these market times?   ask the express market   i won't make
any market markup jokes   as i've done those before   but look
at this religious syncretism   spirituality knows no commonality
i'm looking for my street orchestra   i'm looking for my details
inside   i'm lookin for my inside   my annex   whatever's hidden
behind my furniture   the imprimatur of memory   save me
save me   poetry   with your radio service   your promise of

transmission and redemption   the office of your medicine   i
want to park in your lot   beautifully emptying   empty of
meaning   oh poetry   and honor you   with my knickknacks
and bric-a-brac and   holla back at your beauty   as best i can
it's always transit time   around these parts   i know i'm not
going to white plains   i'm not even sure   what the fuck wasaic
is   wassa i see?   a chair?   this is a nice chair   a chair from
which to view   the trains departing   their fitful starting   i'm
still smarting   from whatever it is   i'm tortured by   in all my
poet's cheesiness   predictable uneasiness   there is a train   of
thought somewhere here   that bridges   new york capital bank
with el rancho   all banks   are dude ranches   i'm in tremont
dude   somehow we got   from no trespassing   to bike lanes
we're back to the real city   the one with traction beyond the
contractors   frank's city   the city of sports shops   the city both
uniform and not   the city where people meet your gaze   the
city where i wander   i can't make up my mind   should i go up
or down tremont   all the way down to concourse perhaps   i'll
go wherever   the city takes me   lunch specials and atms   by
the webster hotel   can't miss adal ramones in concert   can't miss
white horse   for $22.99   or the croissanwich   at two for four
dollars   and chicken fries   yum!   masterminds of cityscape
and popeye's   oh papa yes!   oh papayas!   oh papayes!   it's
getting cold   i don't know   where to go   i should've gone the
other way   more accurate   faster   values of the city   sending
my global mails   my text poems   headed down carter avenue
haven't been this way in a while   a city is always outsize   for
rent perhaps inevitably   i'm running out of things to say   i hope
you enjoy just looking   just hooking on to the city   through the
act of walking   watching my mind's engine   try to clean itself
auto-repair itself   auto itself   redundant   the fritura truck
might be time to bring this show to a close   j'ai une autre chose
à faire   time to eat   time to beat   the city   it all ends in
music   it all ends in improvised song   end of day   parking
auto tech   autotune anthem   anthem of space i name   amid
the 7 elevens   and the food trucks   and the car washes   the
act of walking   the act of talking   the walkie talkie   there's
no wiki for this   halfway through the weekend i'm weak   but
there's no end   to my song

Study for "Everything"

Tenure schmenure the sages are all on the Hudson River pier.
  Don't lean over too far.
I wouldn't be surprised to see arms and legs, even a vital organ
    or two
representing the shy – passive-aggressive – inner life.
Brushing out followed by. . . brushing in.

If people in high-rises shouldn't groan
neither should the brownstones huddle closer together
each time there's a hint of autumn in the air or in the trees –
like, if you'll pardon me for saying so,
rushing to cremate the dead when everyone,
themselves included, knows we want them around for as long as
    humanly possible.

Not, of course, that the pangs have much choice
regarding where to settle, or be observed.
A rusty hydrant is as good as a park bench.
The handful of pigeons poking around a chunk of baguette near
    the grass
don't seem to agree, but they're hand-stamped,
inks (some line, too?) already beginning to fade.

I only know what I know is one version.
Another - as witness so many royal portraits –
or the parade of experimental drugs
for a dread disease – is that knowledge works only some of the
    time.
Really works. Never mind how things
seem as opposed to how they see themselves, or why
appearance stakes so much if not everything on the distinction.

Ambivalent by Nature

Nothing holds me to anything.
Or I want fifty things at once.
– Fernando Pessoa

To go there is easy.
There are moving vans that run only
San Francisco to New York City, and back again.
And in Marin County, so much beauty can be depressing –
driving to the tennis club, the hiking trail, after that
the independent organic grocer where sunlight splashes
the integrated color concrete floor. Where golden rays
seep through bedroom shades, even on gloomy days.
Floor-to-ceiling glass walls, and gardens –
an ocean trail always there, a mountain that circles all around.
Where ardent persons place their homes
to take it in – the whole world rimmed in trees.
Beauty everywhere, and nothing to compare it to,
as we spoil it
with our cars (few trains),
our garbage (on the freeways),
our tents (small cities),
and (are we spoiled?).

Whereas New York City is hard, made by, and for, us –
each tall building built to blot more sun, make more wind
to create its own weather on the sidewalk below, and where most
flowers –
from bougainvillea to narcissus – grow on a roof or hang vertical
in a lobby on Park Avenue. In the parks, each boulder, each tree,
the lampposts, all placed by the landscaper's hand, who is either
famous
or anonymous, as all New Yorkers tend to be.
Timeless and populous, the people, the trash –
its colonies of rats, the Egyptian tomb at the Met –
great civilization now behind glass.

New York is ravaged at the edges,
but firm at its core, the city most like religion –
judgment with complicity,
attractive and repulsive –
something to fight against, or for
with teeth, bone, head, heart.

Letter from Brooklyn

All my life I feared death. Passionately, dutifully, sardonically, silently. But when it came, nothing changed.

I still brush my teeth, worried the cinnamon dental floss will snag in a back molar. A nose hair protrudes. I can feel it between my thumb and forefinger but I can't see it, no matter how I angle my face to the mirror. I dress in the clothes on top of the hamper. My shoes pinch.

I walk the dog on Eastern Parkway in the lightest of snows. If anything, I'm more present, focused on the leash, alert to yank him back from the things he loves in the gutter – a bloody tampon, the yellow intricate intestine that must have been a squirrel once.

My neighbor Dolmatov is doling out peanuts to a flock of sparrows. They swoop in from nowhere, ignoring the dog's outraged stare. The ones in front gobble – *me! Me!* The ones in back puff themselves up, flaunting the faint oil-slick iridescence of their wings. Their polls glisten with a sheen of sleet. Dolmatov rolls each kernel in his fingers and chooses the recipient: *you* and *you*. With his free hand he cracks the shells. His ample belly props him against his walker.

"Snowy enough for you?" he asks. Like all neighbors, he knows nothing of death.

On the next block they are converting a padlocked factory into condos, working on Sunday in bitter cold. High silhouettes in flimsy parkas race across scaffolding, shouting jokes in Nahuatl or Bengali.

The child on his skateboard whizzes past me, close as he knows – *there is no distance! Distance is mine!* It takes all my strength to rein the dog in.

Always when I was alive "life was elsewhere," in a notebook washed blank in the laundromat, in a glance returned from the tinted window of a passing SUV. Perhaps death is also elsewhere?

The little Haredi girl wants to pet the dog – furtively, conscious of breaking a law – and the dog strains forward, fascinated. Fascinated! Is that the only change? That and the swiftness of the clouds, passing from Jersey to the Verrazano in a heartbeat?

At night here are the tenements of my childhood. A single lit window reigns, making the city so vast, so empty. The face that shines there, always in profile – is that my father?

All my life I waited for you, passionately, bitterly, in silence, counting the breaths.

A Train Away

I was on the D
Heading south
Out of the *Boogie Down*
I had a book
It was very good
It was James Elroy
I fell in love with verses
And with escapades
The train came to a *halt*
@ the station
I looked up
Across from me there was a hobo
He too was reading a book
He was in love with verses & escapades
I immediately understood our disease
Verses & escapades
It was like drugs & alcohol
Took us away from our lives
Took us away from the pain of our lives
Took us away from the *Boogie Down*
Took us away from the people on the train
A mere human sea of orbs clouded by mountain mist

The train stopped @ 59th Street and Columbus Circle
I tucked my dog-eared James Elroy into my coat pocket
Got off the D onto the platform
And headed to a poetry reading

Assisted Revolution

(in Central Park)

The faces of granite sculptures in transitory loneliness
Sad interlocked trees hang over benches
Flowers disturb the textures of footprints and hoofmarks
A long-haul chess man receives the call of an apprehensive spring

Pandemic masks, outfits of doom
Mask robbers unite, the future is yours
Shot three times and a booster
Anonymous face-shielded heads and pandemic shoes

Revolution by post-pandemic sex desires
An effortless flow through the bridges of eyes
Stuffed horses pull carriages sheepishly
While bikers snake along the path

There is no melody in the string of noises
It is a sad afternoon of wounded souls
The melted remnants of daylight chained forever to water
Birds chat savage mad love by the fountain

Small boats and ducks are lost in the wind
All compete in arousing colors under sunlight
It's a touch of grace in the sound of bird talk
On the other side of the space-time continuum

The Tearing of the Night

For Frank Simone and Alan Vega

This is the time to fasten. This is the time for boulders, rind. This is the time for Francis Torn. Here is the home of the border.

New York, New York. A scoop of star. A town to straddle, streets to stride. Liberty, a library of eyelid, blossom. And the people, and the people, all the people, c'mon. They are flying, they are striding, they are ours.

Remember Francis, remember Francis, remember Francis Simone.

Hold the dolls, hold their heads. Hold the glory and the newborn air. Hold the Parkside, the JujoMukti. Hold Francis. Hold Francis. Hold Francis Simone.

A man who strode, the rooms he built, rumors birthed. The stars shift corrected. Witness star gloss on the star bones of starry New York. C'mon. The dead pan for fallen stars, shine as the man strides, making and marking his pieces with peace. The barter and batter of words return. C'mon, leave nowhere, meet New York. Francis is flying, he is striding, he is ours.

Oh, this is the time to fasten, and the border is steam-grey blue. Hold the blood of the poet Francis. The piebald Frank. Believe. Believe. Believe. He's a border town. He's a boundary, foundry, quandary, and a quarrel. Welcome, welcome, welcome stranger to Francis Frankie Frank Simone.

Bring advice to the thief and the mucker. Reveal how advice balances sound. The weight and the waiting and forgiving again. And the sound of the sound of the sound of additional sound and the source and silence of this sound and the land and the city and watch this man stride and then fly. Aaaah.

You are a big dog in a big city. Believe. Believe. Believe. Believe in the spark. Believe in speed, in diamond. Dismembered stupidity. Francis, believe in us. This is the time to fasten. Hellfire among us. This is the time to tighten or tear. The land cannot swim. Are you alive, Francis? Run like drunken flesh. Night sky is acme. Rain is midnight food. The space between mirror and thought. The space between mirror and vinegar. The space between mirror and the fool.

New York darkness contains no space. Hold Francis, hold Francis. Hold Francis Frank Simone. The moon fits tight inside you. You are a drummer. Tonight is tight. Border time, Frankie. Francis, you're nearing the border. Francis. Saint Francis. Saint Francis of Assassin. The last apple in the afterlife. Aaaah Aaaah.

My father's friends included Sid Seed and Nellie Rottenberry. I know Gass Wild, Billy Cancel, Julie Unruly, Jennifer Blowdryer, and Puma Perl. It's all rock n roll, Frankie. It's all rock n roll. The city is fighting and it rocks and it rots. Bloodhounds, blood poets. Poison and fire storm. City of jest. Swayfarers, stragglers, smugglers, jugglers, girls with clout and guilt. Fray merchants, justifiers, men with arms stuck to their sides. The colon moves to your heart. Fasten, fasten, and rise. Oh Francis, oh Francis. How did you survive the moon?

Night falls to its death. Light suckles its mother. C'mon, c'mon. This heartbeat world of New York. This striding town in its striding boots. This turf, this cord, this spine, this frost and frosting. This past on past on past buried and bedded and waiting. Bride-light for the citizens. Clamber city.

Frankie, have you left the border yet? Wayfarer, do you believe punk rock failed? Do you believe in honey? Con-fetti-fusion? This is one time fasten. This is the one time for boulders. New York is poised, a rolling, a breathing, is melody. Padded to miracle wish.

The forest is forest-green, the city is cacophony. New York, New York. A scoop of star for Frank. Frankie Frankie Frank Simone. Swallow this sound. Hold, hold, hold the street in your hand and believe.

One day the rivers will be damned. The final letter of the last departed on the brink of the water at the edge of this town. Of the last grip of the hand of the cusping figure that strides the curving air and the drift of the land and the heel and the lintel of the land and each and every room in this land of the land. This is forever, this city is us. Mud ghosts and glitter merchants. C'mon, New York, c'mon, c'mon.

Crosstown

Back in New York I grab a taxi at Port Authority,
A young Jamaican guy, then a big Af-Am guy in
A monster silver SUV tries to cut him off but he dashes
Round in front like a fox and then can't move
So we're sitting in the traffic people leaning
On their horns all around us and the big guy comes
Out and starts threatening my driver – I'm just out
Of jail. – So go back to jail. No love lost it happens
All the time, They think they are tough and we are
Nothing, we think they are worse than nothing.
He's been driving two years saving to go to school
To catch up on his computer design skills, the wife
Got impatient and cheated on him, he still sees his
Little daughter who is so pretty and smart she can
Read at the age of four. He'd like to be a better
Christian but working this job he gets in situations
Where he uses bad language. Next day another
Cabbie this one older we talk about Iraq and about power
I say we are seeing the defects of democracy
He says he doesn't believe in democracy democracy
Is for the rich.

Went to Sheila's, we walked on Riverside Drive as
The sun was setting bathing the high limbs of the elms
Coral, the trunks sinking into darkness, we were
Happy together and other walkers also looked happy
Trees tranquilly surviving blight seemed fine
A man passed us with a poodle so elegant it looked
Like a model on a runway.

Small kid on the crosstown bus, a high clear voice:
If you kick somebody, people won't be your friend.
Woman next to me carries a large flat manila envelope

Her makeup is violent her middle-aged hair is lacquered
Her coat olive green embroidered cashmere expensive
I think art? photography? then I see the envelope says
X-rays, so it's cancer.

Two Poems

New York City

A man is a woman
& a woman is a man

Only when you hide your face,
the world reveals itself
clearly to you.

Human hipbones,
harder than those iron fences,
wind swifter, wiser & faster
than fish bones do.

Troubles; pranks; tricks.

A woman is a man
& a man is a woman
& feet are minds
& eyes are feet.

"Where is today's catch?"

Bar – New York City

Don't shout!
Speak easy in a hush!
A jukebox, shining like a monolith,
serenades a popular song
of our youth.

Let's fool ourselves thinking
it's not drinks that we want,
but the shaded interior

of "somewhere" where
the sun doesn't reveal
the details of our lives
too cruelly.

Let's speak in a dry whisper,
pretending that the sticky floors & a cloudy mirror
suit our desire well to be left alone.

Let's act as if we were proud & civil,
not sullen & disproportioned.

Let's enjoy the dark daydreaming
together believing that
everything is fine & dandy

finally

NEW YORK CITY

AN ATTRACTIVE WOMAN
WITH MAKE UP ON HER FACE
DESIGNER CLOTHES
AND HIGH HEELS
CROSSING THE STREET
ON A RED LIGHT
SOPHISTICATED AND SASSY
A SWITCHBLADE FOR A TONGUE
NEVER SMILING
ALWAYS SERIOUS
NEW YORK CITY
A MAN WHO WANTS TO BE A BOY
PLAY MORE THAN WORK
DREAM MORE THAN CREATE
THERE IS A SOUL THERE
TRYING TO CONNECT WITH OTHER SOULS
WHO ARE WANDERING THROUGH THE MAZE
OF STEEL AND STONE
LIVING EIGHT HOURS A DAY
IN A COFFIN WITH GADGETS AND SCHEDULES
LOOKING FOR SOMETHING REAL
AT LUNCH TIME
NEW YORK CITY
A BUNCH OF CHILDREN
HANGING OUT ON THE CORNER
PLOTTING THEIR NEXT SCHEME
PLANNING ANOTHER PRANK
PLAYING MONOPOLY WITH FAKE MONEY
BELIEVING IT'S A GOD THING
TO BUY AND SELL
IS ALL THAT MATTERS
LIFE IS NOT IN THE MARKET
JUST RATIONALIZED
HOW TO CAPITALIZE
IS THE PRIZE
NEW YORK CITY
A PUBLIC ZOO
WHERE EXOTIC ANIMALS
FROM ALL OVER THE WORLD

ARE CAPTURED
PUT IN A CAGE
GIVEN A STAGE
TO ACT OUT THEIR PARTS
ENTERTAIN THE VISITORS
TRY TO GET ALONG
UNTIL THEIR FOOD IS POISONED
THEY BLAME EACH OTHER
DIDN'T KNOW THE ZOOKEEPER
WAS STILL IN CHARGE
DIDN'T KNOW THEY HAD THE KEY
TO UNLOCK THEIR OWN CAGE
AND BE FREE
NEW YORK CITY
A CHILD'S GAME
RED LIGHT GREEN LIGHT ONE TWO THREE
HOP SCOTCH
JUMPING DOUBLE DUTCH
DANCING ON THE SUBWAY
PLAYING PATTY CAKE
AT THE BUS STOP
DOING A WHEELIE
ON A DIRT BIKE
IN THE MIDDLE OF TRAFFIC
THROWING ROCKS IN CENTRAL PARK
CHASING SQUIRRELS UP A TREE
NEW YORK CITY
PANDORA'S BOX
A SOCIAL EXPLOSION
A SPIRITUAL TIME BOMB
GOD HAS BEEN BLOWN UP
ALL OVER THE PLACE
HE BE BLACK
HE BE WHITE
HE BE SHE
HE BE RIGHT
HE'S IN CONTROL OF OUR SOULS
THERE ARE STORIES UNTOLD
NO MATTER WHAT HIS OR HER NAME
THE IDEA IS TO KEEP YOU SANE
LEARN TO LIVE IN SUCH A WAY
WE'LL ALWAYS SEE A BRIGHTER DAY

Dog

The New York streets look nude and stupid
With Ted and Edwin no longer here
To light them up with their particularity
Of loving them and with intelligence
In some large sense of the word:
New York's lost some of its rough charm
And there's just no getting around it
By pretending the rest of us can somehow make up for it
Or that future generations will. I hear
A dog barking in the street and it's drizzling
At 6 a.m. and there's nothing warm
Or lovable or necessary about it, it's just
Some dog barking in some street somewhere.
I hate that dog.

Supernatural Bread

Lexington Avenue tugged the bus to Easthampton
like a joke dollar bill just out of reach each time
I neared it having missed its stop at 77th, and chased

it to the next which I hoped would be 69th but had to bet
on 66th when the curtain of traffic drew back to show
its brake lights squint, a wounded beast retreating,

but I gave chase as if pursued as well, my zombie failures
on my heels, nostalgic for my undoing, but it wouldn't,
the bus, in fact stop until it reached the curb at 59th,

after I'd slalomed bodies under Hunter College
jet bridge, got beyond the aromatic reach of the Halal
carts and the Greek Grill truck, caterers to the great

experiment in public education as a mist slicked
my rucksack plus the duffel I had packed because
there's no night bus back to Manhattan, and I'd planned

to stay the night out there where it was more like New
England than New York, but borders are imagined
like the difference between tints and tones, and this is

most the case for Easthampton where I'd got a room
in an eighteenth-century farmhouse the restoration of which
was overseen by this owner-guy who offhandedly thanked

his stars, he said, for walls to fend off migrants.
His farm, he said with some restrained self-adulation,
may once have harbored runaways, you know, from

before the Civil War, and I thought to ask him why he'd
euphemize slavery with that shibboleth of history, the War,
but thought again like maybe it would be impolite or petty

to blow spit balls at his house of cards, and so I harbored
in my head the weary travelers chasing liberation which
by nature has to lurch just out of reach each time it gets

precipitously close to revealing itself as the mere abstraction
that it is, but somehow the idea reduced the fugitives' lives
to an allegory of my own as if we'd all together received

all tomorrows' bread in catching the coach that moseyed
down Lex as if, indeed, it were the very pachyderm of time
itself that would have left a bus-shaped door in the rain,

the threshold of the future neither coming into view nor
losing focus, the static hum of connection with only
the infinite in between.

Bushwick Brooklyn

These strangers,
these new faces,
white nuns and priests
gathered like bibles on a shelf,
waiting for me.

A woman applies burned ashes
of coal chalk
underneath my eyes.
They are black and sagging
like everyone else now.

The red eyed sentinels,
scorning me coldly
One of the nuns undresses
my white virgin body,
I am a skinless raccoon.

All the windows have shutters.
Paints of yellow vague moonlight.
Rain on the wall echoes over my skin,
meows scratches, the red cat weeps

Dark and red lilies and crowfoot
are everywhere.
Black crows crying in my eyes,
winds whistling through
these black holes.
My mind is running away,
it won't let me out.

Permanent Marker

After the first Bombing
We had a renovation job, 102nd and 103rd floor
600 pound test on the chilled water
Even the hangers leaked
10 hour days on repeat
More wrench than real life
Sparks are flyin'
"There may be no peace in this Chaos kid,
But there's a payout for sure"
High above New York skyline
Among the men who forgot fear

There were the Jimmies, the Richies,
Mack, Billy, Sal
Mutt & Jeff, side-mouth Singh
And Bucky with his small hands
The way he pawed his mustache when he told a story
Every day there was a story
Bee line to the commuter bar
Lap at the mahogany
That barmaid didn't know what hit her

Back then it was Sativa at 6
And the largest coffee known to man
Shake out the cobwebs
Tighten up loose ends
Ole Timers drinkin' tinis before seven
Tellin' us they never did drugs in their lives
High above Manhattoes bedrock with IM Pei

"You could buy all yaw 'lectronics hea'"
"Vacuum tubes as far as the eye could see"
Thousand stalls – TV parts

A place in time
A time forgotten
Commerce, towering over the Battery

From the north you could see all the way
Up to German Town
To the East, ghost breweries of Brooklyn
Industrial waterfront Queens
To the West, Jersey

Don't recall how it started or who was first
The outlines just started to appear
At coffee break there were one or two
By evening the long narrow window was full
All in permanent marker
Cityscape with Sharpie
"Times was different then, Kid"
"We did all the cold water flats"
"Way after the Dodgers left"
"Before the Chinese bought up the West Side "
With every turn of the pen
This one, he had worked on
Upper East Side
The other, their fathers had built
Looking north past Chelsea

Every boiler
All the chillers
Our fathers and their fathers
"Enough pipe to take you all the way to the moon"
All the bedrock will hold
Once there were gas welders
No one sees this city like we do

*

Behind the first chill, face down
you lower this shade half way
as if the window itself has died

from letting the bedroom do
what it does best, darken
and though the walls are hollow

they have no use for your fingers
already around what once
was the ripcord, yanked

by the instant that never let go
so nights could gather in a group
to stop their descent in time

the way this glass sheet tries
to hide itself from the ground
be seen only as the emptiness

side by side pressing against you
half windshield, half want to die
alone and still missing.

LES: Past and Pandemic

I was a child of Tenth Street
Police locks and bodegas
Open hydrants, rooftops,
cerveza on credit
We were poor and tough,
might have seemed hard,
but if a child stumbled
a hundred hands reached out
to break his fall
In the street, on the stoops,
under tenement skies
We were always home
Everywhere was home.

I was a child of Seventh Street
Tompkins Square Park
was our front yard
Handball and Latin nights,
rock shows on the bandshell,
late nights on the benches
In the morning, we'd clear
the sandbox of syringes
so our kids could play,
chasing each other
past the wooden seesaws
and the metal swings
The Strip, the basketballs
the pills along Ninth Street
"I got the tea that killed Bruce Lee"
at the entrance
The park was home.

I was a child of Third Street
The Nuyorican Poets Café
where I learned
how words could feel
Lines for cocaine
and welfare cheese
Heroin and poetry
Presidential, 357,
baskets lowered
from fifth floor
windows, hands
creeping out of grates
Abandoned buildings
waiting for developers,
kids sleeping under
Star Wars sheets
Three eggs for Thanksgiving
Bacardi for Christmas
The streets were home.

Down here in the Lower,
below Delancey,
below Grand,
I'm no longer a child
The sun rises in my window
Diva and I walk along
the East River some days,
or maybe along South Street
Now and then,
a longer journey
across Houston
I am home
with keys and a couch,
books and television
Empty highways

and ferries
below my window
I am home,
but in these pandemic times
I feel homeless

Those Tenth Street days
flood my memory
and remind me
that everywhere is home,
stoops and streets and rivers,
We are always home.

Poem

after Mayakovsky

In my heart

there is a horse-drawn carriage

that is setting me off

like the siren on a fire-truck

O winter of New York!

how decidedly damp you are!

Gloom stalking through your very many mean streets

As only the light from store-windows illumines

Sidewalk newspaper-vendors.

Two flat

Two in high-heels.   (four feet)

Stepping over puddles

containing whole universes!

Tidal Connections

for Yuko & Karen

as they have for 475 million years
here at Plumb Beach NY
the Limulus Polyphemus emerge
from the depths of the Ocean
the moon driven females spawn & lay their eggs
15,000 to 64,000
the males in tow hitching a ride to spray
shore birds' caviar refueling after a 9000 miles journey
this symbiosis this reliable emergence
brings peace & perspective

to be continued...

depuis 475 millions d'années
ici à Plumb Beach NY
les Limulus Polyphemus émergent
des profondeurs de l'océan
les femelles poussées par la lune fraient et pondent leurs œufs
de 15 000 à 64 000
les mâles accrochés attelés les fertilisent
un caviar pour les oiseaux de rivage migrateurs
qui font le plein après un voyage de 15 000 kms
cette symbiose cette émergence fiable
apporte paix et perspective

à suivre...

Waltzing Nostalgia

now everyday i hear
the bells at st. mark's church
ringing in the hours
and the noise of street traffic,
then party people
occupying the sidewalk
through the night
a new apartment
full of new sounds:
doors slamming in the hall
humming refrigerator
and the arms of a mini art
installation moving on the
mantle: gold painted
prosperity kittens with
their arms constantly waving
and the words: ukraine
shall overcome
& crimea is ukraine
painted on their bodies
i am back in a neighborhood
where i used to live years ago
things are familiar
yet foreign too
i run into old acquaintances
from when these few blocks
held a tribe i felt a part of
or at least dangled on the
edges of or dallied there
but so many places are gone now:
sunshine deli, gargoyle mechanique,
the gas station, the telephone bar,
kiev diner, st. mark's books

all have gone
but I can still visit the same parks:
tompkins square, liz christy garden
all the community gardens
and once in a while gaze
into the same eyes
older but still recognizable

Before the Audition: Times Square, 1990

You sang Broadway songs
nobody wanted to hear.
Flew through the starry city full of
GIRLS, GIRLS, GIRLS!
Central Park wildings, muggers,
cabdrivers with parakeets.
A tube of lipstick in your fist
like blood or prayer.
The *Kiss Me Red* pointing
to your clamshell mouth.

Your hips swayed through Riverside park,
uncurling your face to the sun
You were not stuck yet,
men had names like Guy and Tom,
you felt sorry for all of them,
in your greedy young way.
Their penises shrank and grew in your hands
like mushrooms or flowers.

This was the clockwise track
they smile about years later.
A notch, a mole like you
is never beautiful enough.

Almost Brooklyn

It was a break-up without tears this time, thank God
But that joint we chose to toast our final goodbye was definitely
a mistake
The bartender with his heavy pour
The widow with a seductive view of that historic metaphor of
granite and steel
And since romance has always been the bigger fish than reason
Off we went just couple of bad decisions crossing the sky between
two boroughs

The frigid wind off the East River didn't so much sober us up as
keep us from falling on our ass
Just a bald guy desperately trying to be a hat guy and his Muppet
Baby Courtney Love
We just needed to make it across without international incident
Brooklyn would be closure Brooklyn could bring peace
But the coziness of our silence jabbed at us like a switchblade,
and I just knew she couldn't resist

It was the tone that I recognized before the words
All Chipmunk, chainsaw and child of the damned
"Mikey" the Angel-baby of death inside her growled
"I want you to fuck me right here on the bridge"
"Ok" I said because...well, who's Nancy really without her Sid?

"Ya' got protection, right Mikey?" she asked throwing me the stiff arm
And I did! I fucking did! Tucked deep in the folds of the wallet
she gave me
A forlorn talisman vestiges of my inner delusional 9th grader
But despite the tell-tale discolored leather halo
my rifling fish-stick fingers found no prize.

When I turned to gently break the news
Her answer was a melodic snore her head tipped back like a
broken Pez dispenser
Brooklyn was off the menu
Our evening closed with a classic rerun
A broken stiletto hurled at my head
A screamy dust up at an Ave A ATM
The map of our doomed relationship written across her face in
lines of smeared mascara

Awoke much later with that dirty concussed vampire feeling
The robotic *"You have no messages"* felt like a declaration of victory
Its own kind of peace
Hungry from a night of almosts I reached for my wallet to buy
some New Double Dragon
And damn if it wasn't right there
right between my Kim's Video card and my lucky 2 dollar bill
Halleluiah! Protected after all

On the Money Train

on the money train
on the honey train
on the gravy train
this is a gravy stain
what is there to say?
I take the fifth
I take the fourth
I take the D train
I take the A and the C
down from the heights
up from the village
over from Jersey
where I lived with my dad
in my first year at Columbia
dad slept in the kitchen by a gas stove
in the middle of winter
I froze in the front
but nothing phased me
tough as nails
in my dream to conquer worlds
but the dream I have now
is my dad's sacrifice for so many years
to help his sons.

Brooklyn

This poem for Brooklyn
is about you   it is never
about I   it is never
they or them or it
or us
it is you
and always has been

Down these concrete steps
narrow streets alleys
wide avenues parkways
parks seem to go
back
back one hundred years
before there was cobblestone
dirt lanes crossed everywhere

God the eagle has soared
and landed in Brooklyn
this thing you call Brooklyn
moonscape landscape building scape
fire and fire escape

Brooklyn Eagle   Walt Whitman
wonder of science   There is no art
to it To this landing
to this falling
down stoops
and broken pavement
steps and
broken concrete

How can you say this is Brooklyn
when it's not
How can you say endless
when it's that

Oak and elm and flowering cherry
glacial ravine, rock out cropping
overpass and under pass
squirrel and pizza,   squirrel
eating pizza I swear no one would believe
it   and you Blackbird   trying so hard
to get into my poem

Ode to the Orange Bear

I'd arranged the poetry reading for October,
but the Orange Bear, where the reading took place,
was on Murray Street, in the financial district,
only blocks from where the World Trade Center towers
had collapsed in fire and rubble only a month before.

We moved the reading up to mid-January.
I took the Metroliner up from Maryland,
my friend Roger meeting me at Penn Station.
We stopped at his office on 53rd Street,
skyscraper windows looking south, downtown.
"I had to look away," Roger confessed. "I couldn't watch."
Of course, we'd all see it over and over again
on television for months to come.

We rode the subway downtown,
emerging like moles into daylight and snow,
a smell of ash and smoke like an invisible shroud,
four months later, the snow
reinforcing the tomblike solemnity.
Tourists milled around the fenced-off crater
where the buildings once stood.

In the Orange Bear, we met Pepper, the host,
who sponsored us to a scotch.
Cigarette smoke hazed the room,
city ordinances be damned, and over
the mahogany bar a cheap painting
of a reclining odalisque hung
like the cover of a pulp fiction novel; a broken-down
pool table in the center of the room
likewise reinforcing the mood.

The first poet, a humanitarian activist,
read poems about tortured children,
raped women, Central American military thugs,
so fitting to the World Trade Center atmosphere.

Then it was my turn.
Already looking forward to my train home,
I stood behind the microphone
by the wobbly billiards table.

New York City – Part Two

Again into your guts
into your belly
    that receives me,
stoic I make my way
through the crowd.
    I arrive to you
and you throw me
a bite of hope
that keeps me alive,
gives me a bit of calm.
With shamed words
I return to your mouth
that opens and repeats
a promise to me.
City that urges me
    to tell it all
to observe it all:
news proclaimed
in its moment under
the bench of a random station,
an older woman dressed
in white who preaches
    the apocalypse
with the hysteria
of the abandoned.
    Siren city,
unending chant,
compels me to stop,
    I tie myself
to the memories,
I die each night
in your night,
but it is not my time

and I return to the voice
of your chaotic beat,
banquet city inhabited
by many a Tantalus,
stone upon which
I build my hell each day,
I carry you on my back,
I push you to the summit,
entire city that crashes
     down about me.

Let's Move

I don't like it
You get close
Then they go
It's the city
It's too hard
They get more
Someplace else
I start thinking
I'm leaving, too.
Every year I fixate
On that new somewhere
My mind is busy packing boxes
Deciding what color to paint the new walls
Picturing the car I'll park in the driveway
I zip through Zillow
Finding perfection
In the places I've never been
Where future neighbors are the strangers
I'll stare at from the kitchen window
I'll have two cats and a dog
A lawn I don't know how to tend
A vegetable garden I forget to water
A septic tank
A leaking roof
An astronomical heating bill
No.
I'll take noisy streets
Ageism
The infiltration of the suburban-minded rich
The no-yard
No car
Concrete
Pockets of stench

Dirty buses
Crowded subways
Mouse infestations
Caved in ceilings
Greedy landlords
The swim upstream

After *Red Noir*

for Anne Waldman

There is something about NYC
that makes you feel life will
go on forever despite

everything we have done
to ourselves or that others
have done to us. You get

that feeling even while riding
in a subway car (in the
Paris Métro too) with everyone

coming and going around you
or when seeing what must
be one of the most beautiful

creatures on earth stretch
out before you or take
your hand to lead you to

a place where you can get
a better view of all that
is unfolding before you.

In the Tunnel

Not much fun to be working in the tunnel,
when you could be on the train,
heading somewhere interesting, like Far Rockaway,
a place you've never been.

But here you are, supervising guys in Day-Glo vests,
directing them because you are the engineer.
You are the one who builds the tracks
and makes the trains run on schedule.

You get so bored you sit on a rail,
prop your chin on your hand, and fall asleep...
until you hear the blast of a horn in your ear
and see the glaring headlight of a waiting train.

The motorman leans out his small window
and yells, "You're on the wrong track!"
And you see how close you've come to oblivion
by resting yourself on the railroad to ruin.

Joy Drives His Life

for Steve Dalachinsky

You were the guy who could write a poem on your way to your next
    reading
& read it without fear when you arrived.
I remember you included me just because I was front row with camera
& you could say hello so you put me in a seat on the train next to you.
Hello... you're alive... in my poem.

you'd come around like the new jazz
to sing another song of freedom... & free was not square

Impossible now to not have you here

when I think of Japanese forest bathers I think of you

you bathed in the ailanthus shade on Spring Street,
under sycamores along the Seine you were sure to walk
willows in Giverny wept for you & Yuko.
Soaked in a thunderstorm in Louisville, under live oaks our 1st
real conversation, crowded into Phil's dry van on our way to Ron
Whitehead's Insomniacathon,
the MC worried you would never hold to your allotted 5 minutes.

Impossible now to not have you here

you were never one of the shy ones
I remember you asked as you walked off stage
(it was the Bowery Poetry Room/ Nesenkeag Farm benefit)
no Steve you did not hog the mike
thank you for starting up the show.

Impossible now to not have you here

or at the Gershwin Hotel, or Farm Day, or inside Lowell's Grotto
did you know it's no longer there?
(the landlord sold the Gem Spa sign too)

on Metro North train down to Grand Central Station
a ticket to ride to your Memorial

"seen through a scruff of trees & vegetation which grow on
periphery of an industrial site, Hudson River"
writ with hand swept aerosol paint
call it appropriation/call it Basquiat graffiti:

LIVE ONLY TWICE.

Poseurs

The hammer pounding
into the street is pretentious,
asserting superiority over the asphalt
that it shatters into chaos.
Pretentious cars bounce
over holes in the street,
as if they couldn't fall in
if one was big enough.
Dumb people think they own the street
while the sidewalk sarcastically sparkles
beneath their feet. The sidewalk is
pretentious, thinking it rivals the stars.
But the stars are phonies, too.
A few billion years ago they were snuffed out,
and now are mere hangovers
from long-gone events –
incompetent multitudes pretending to divide
the infinite night sky. Infinity is also
a bullshit artist. Outside the infinite set
are sets of infinite sets. And so on.

The Cannoli Machine at the Brooklyn Detention Center

The cannoli machine in the Brooklyn Detention Center is for the
visitors;
my dad waited in line when he went to visit my brother.
He didn't know he'd have to empty his pockets,
take off his pinky ring, and untie his shoes.
This is the first time I saw my father afraid,
but he wasn't too afraid to stand in line
with all the other fathers
in front of the cannoli machine.
He ate two or three and noticed a little white cream filling on
his cheek
when he saw himself on the surveillance camera;
he noticed that his white t-shirt was washed too many times
and was starting to turn grey,
that his socks didn't match.
I didn't know this was how fathers were made.

It's Not the Heat

Two choices: Make it to the bar, and pee,
Or drop your fake leather PU pants
Just enough – just open
The car door, yeah, open
The back door too and just do it.

Make sure there are no schools, within 100 feet is it?
Don't want to be the literal poster girl
For aging poets who don't quite
Have it down, need relief in this

Desert, but aren't quite cute enough anymore.
But, I can still cop a squat, so I do.

NYC in the heat is like a dog's breath when
They get too close. Waiting for the grate of
Tongue, then drip, then the lingering. In a whiff. Beats. It's not
Like this street – It's *not called* Avenue B for nothing is it?

Nah, They just ran out of Avenue A's so here
We are stuck with B's. By the sacred Ganges.

Avenue B, where blades of grass are actually
Growing in tree boxes now. Primped
As the curls in the most distressed of

Black leather pants.
Eye lashes. Being separated. As if they were

Religious leaders, arguing,
On the head of that holy pin.

Great Jones

"Is anyone here familiar with Page Six?'
queries the fresh-faced tour guide
As his audience dutifully snaps
phone shots of Basquiat's last address
now tackily smeared in corny graffiti, bearing no semblance
to the dead master's jazzy hieroglyphics
My block now a sightseeing stop
Replete with an earnest hipster guide - proud city resident
of a dozen years
who jauntily references the New York Post
to people doubtlessly cooler than him,
even if they do live out of town
Because with all his freshly minted street smarts
You know he's no native
Never known the thrill of your first independent subway trip,
undiscovered by parents
or sought Millay's lyrical ghost on teenaged ferry rides
ending in wonton soup's steaming solace
How every block and each hood inscribed in history and heart
Unaware that the faux and freshly painted couplet, "If you Can Dream It,
You Can Do It"
A bogus echo to brand bohemianism
Saccharine slogan for this well-intentioned tour

Caruso Sweating & Big Nick in His Underwear

on the hottest days of summer
when everybody's windows
were open wide
he'd come around:
an old Italian wino
sweating beneath a heavy wool
overcoat 4 sizes too large.

he used to roam the backyards
between the tenement buildings
& sing
great songs
in italian
with a clear & powerful voice.
& people would lean out windows
& throw money. kids would sit
with their legs hanging over fire
escapes with their mouths open.

when he was finished the old
man would bend over like a bird
& pick up coins & fill the
pockets of his great overcoat.

sometimes when big nick was home,
drinking beer in his underwear,
he'd yell down to him, bravo!
bravo! ... hey caruso, here! & he'd
throw out a fistful of singles.
& the old man with sweat running
down his face would stand under
his window & pour out his soul
and sing nick's favorite:
male femmena.

& many of the women would cry.
& the sun would shine down
through the hot muggy
summer & it would rain
money in the backyards.

Leaving New York City

Walking uptown after work, standing in a crowd
on the corner – the extreme West Side near the highway,
or a little further downtown,
where twenty years ago the towers came down –

I was waiting at a crosswalk for the light to change
when I caught sight of a silver jetliner from LaGuardia
lumbering windward over the lucid stacks of Midtown.
As I watched it ascend at an awkward angle,

sunlight flashing off its fuselage, it got stuck
in a long moment in my memory, like a photograph
embedded in a film, and for a minute or two,
as if in a trance, I realized

I wasn't breathing anymore or my heart beating.
Sometimes it happens like this – you die, almost
invisibly, an outline in chalk,
pedestrians looking down at their phones

while managing to politely step over or around you.
When I lived in New York I always wanted to leave –
then, after being away awhile, burned to get back
to the maw of city streets, the din

of traffic's exhaustive rush to nowhere.
But at this moment I thought I was gone for good,
and might have tarried there awhile like a ghost, or as one
would have in the late 19th Century, with cane and top hat

marveling at the progress of industry –
brick and ironwork façades

of new buildings going up almost overnight –
the invasion of electricity and streetcars dialing up

and driving the pace in which civilization's cranked
toward the future.
As the light changed and I began to shuffle forward,
head-on into the reflection of sunlight on steel, this

contemporaneous now,
I took a noisy swallow of air and woke up
to the familiar claw of desire, the insatiable ache for
the truth I wanted but knew I'd never have.

Evening in Gravesend

The older men of Ocean Parkway
appear like daylight fades,

a slow and deliberate stirring,
standing around a pair of dice

and some colored markers as if
these tools were the flint

that some imaginary pit of fire
built to keep the memory warm.

If it's true that time does, indeed,
move faster as we get older,

and if it's true that the machine
we've built collapses as we age,

that a year, a month, a moment
means not what it used to mean,

if we are forgetting the distances
of an afternoon or evening's miles,

then let these men embrace speed,
let them extend their glorious wings

and take flight – these proud, caped –
and race the bandit across the sky.

Immediate City

Tall and plural and parallel,
their buff, excited skins
of glass pressed to glass and steel
bronzed by the falling sun,
the city's figmentary buildings dream
that they are one with the One.
Ignoring the office workers
trapped inside their neural nets,
they orient their ecstasy
up past the circling jumbo jets.
Older than the rocks is she

across whom their shadows float.
A million rivers navigate
the necklace at her throat.
The light that falls and falls
shatters in her million prisms.
In one of her million cubicles,
a man tunes his inner mechanisms,
types an endless memorandum.
Time moves slowly, then not at all.
A boy and two girls are
trading secrets down the hall.

Manhattan Sapphics

Grist and gum give texture to subway platforms.
Air Force 1 OGs are the hot new platforms.
High, a guy shouts, "White people suck," his platform
Pitt and Delancey.

No one's rich except all the rich. The Wall Street
folk have fled to Quogue, while the broke will stoop-sit
chanting old-school prophecies: get your chop cheese
sandwich to go, please.

Ah, New York, you polarize, rank choice, trash talk.
Which is cheaper? Uber or yellow taxi?
Even dreams have sharpened their discord like a
penthouse foreclosure.

Smell the Bad Old Days in the garbage heaped on
dumpsters, say clairvoyants with sketchy assets.
Smell the Good Old Days, say the once-were club-kid
junkies for Warhol.

Hope

an open letter to posterity from a minor poet of the 21st century

Moondog said it long ago... Bye bye bye Manhattan
So long Steve Dalachinsky and Steve Cannon
the Grassroots Tavern and Carnegie Deli
St. Mark's Books and Sidewalk Café
Say adios to living in a zip that starts with 1
Can we hope again to afford a Yankees game,
a Broadway play or a taxi ride across town?
Where have all the people gone?

This is for you Larry Kelly fighting, fighting, fighting
for breath on the whirring ventilator of fate.
What can we say about hope when there isn't hope?
We can say: It's time to get to work, to clean up the mess
 we have left our children and our children's children
as well as our parents' generation so we are seen
in a kinder light by history and any god
who takes an interest in the daily lives of human-kind.

We must retrain ourselves to look for the good
in fellow humans not just mistakes and moments
of weakness. We need to remind ourselves the
measure of life is the journey undertaken
not the rewards we accrue at any given time.
We as a species can still achieve wonders
when pushed and we are pushed in ways
not seen in generations. We need compassion

and community action while living in isolation
and distance by necessity and choice. The screens
we're addicted to offer little solace to the lonely
mortals we've become in spite of our strength
as social creatures who once upon a time

enjoyed each other's company. Time passes
like clouds through a sleepless night haunted
by fever dreams of those we've left behind.

The sirens passing by the front of our home
as common as the chirping of the birds in back.
The morning news infuriates because we know
our president is ill equipped to deal with a cisirs
that wouldn't be as bad if he wasn't around.

Everyone I know is in the process of losing
someone dear to them. I wake up every few hours
with my chest beating wondering who's next?

Every cough is not the end, every breath precious.
A walk outside the house should not be occasion
for an argument with Caroline. I've caught up on
reading back copies of the New Yorker and know
as much about Bolivian politics and Fiona Apple's
mental state as I'll ever need to know. My neighbor,
a kindly woman is shouting at passersby
"wear a mask, don't be an asshole."

I have phoned my Brooklyn teacher friends
and empathized with the conundrum of online
teaching while schooling one's own children home
from school. We have come to learn that quarantine
is not a romantic proposition.
There's a time for metaphor and a time for reality
and this shit is real in a way we've rarely seen.
The opposite of hope is despair with fear as a catalyst
favored by demagogues and their shady minions.

Our survival is unsustainable if we dread each other
though right now we must protect ourselves from each

other by distance and social responsibility.
Facebook nostalgia may serve as balm
but hope is the only cure
because without hope none of this matters
without hope none of this mattered.

The Monster Lives of Boys & Girls

omni omni homonym
omni humanym
omni anima
omni immortalis
omni rushtophil & rushing
omni manatee & mandible
omni omnibus, tell me

am I the daughter of a city
or am I the daughter
of a man?

This urban wrapped rose, dog rose wrapped
in particulate air, where flies

an urban bumble bee and all, and the female sparrow, adept
at aphid picking, comes to feed amidst delphinium on
    Avenue B

    Ho, sparrows, knocking the petals
off flowers, leaves
    of trees, tell

how to display
the monster lives of boys & girls
strutting in finery down Avenue A

As you know, I'm writing this for you and you only, mutant,
all these little details I put in for you — this man
sweating in blue stocking & red leotard suit, he's got it
backwards, that grid of this world
that shows the mute web of human endeavor   kissing
animals & plants

This word, the word "hierarchy"
the word "summer"
summer summer summer thunder, thief,
thief, thief in the night it's something
you love, it's here
only for you

Round about Midnight

for linda jones

there is a point
between night & day
where it all comes clear
& bright, a new beginning

where yesterday
can be left behind
& a new day is there
to greet us, clean

with promise
& a clear path
thru the hours before dawn
when the mind kicks in,

the squares all tucked in bed
& the people of the night
in charge of the scene – players,
musicians, whores,

countermen at diners & cats
delivering the morning papers,
garbagemen & cops & drunks
in the rhythms of midnight

& the small hours after,
a different sphere completely
from daytime, traffic
& the peculiar world of commerce –

this is when the music is made,
in nightclubs until two

or four a.m., & then in after-
hours joints & people's cribs,

or in the recording studios
after the gig, with everyone nice
& relaxed, half-
juiced or lazy,

hazy, a little crazy maybe
but ready to put down some tunes
onto recording discs or tape
for the rest of the world to hear –

round midnight & after, the end
of a day, or in the meta-
phorical mode, it's the last sigh
of an era, like around 1939

thru '44, with the war
going on abroad & the nation
finally tearing itself loose
from the last dying grip

of pre-modern america,
all its young men at war
& only the rejects, mis-
fits & draft-dodgers left

to shape some new form
from the ruins of the past,
some measure of their alienation
from the day before,

their allegiance to the flag
of tomorrow, like whatever

it might bring would be better
than what's happening right now,

the high discovery
of risk, or the existential premise
that something new & brilliant can be made
from the existing materials,

the intention
"to create & invent
on little jobs" that monk
spoke of in 1948, with no reward

but the beauty of the thing itself,
the challenge of invention
with no idea of what might come next,
no pattern to fall back on,

nothing but the driving force in-
side yourself, & the long roots of culture
stretching back to west Africa
& the southern united states,

the utter & absolute beauty
of making a bridge
across the years, to link the past
in a whole new way

with what would come next,
round about midnight
of a dying world & round about
3 a.m. of a brand new day,

monk at the piano
composing the future

& bud powell taking the piece
to cootie williams to record,

1944, a standard of modern music
even before its composer could record it,
the loveliest work in modern jazz
at just over three minutes long

yet longer than tomorrow,
longer than the 45 years
since monk eased it out of his head
& his gargantuan heart

& gave it to us,
"round about midnight," as a sign
that something was coming
that had never been here before

Schism

Today in the taxi a passenger got in and she was crying. I don't
    know why. We left
Astoria for Williamsburg. I gave her a little package of tissues
    and she went on her way.
Kafka said *crying is especially alarming for me. I cannot cry. When
    other people cry, it*
seems to me like a strange, incomprehensible natural phenomenon.

I thought maybe she was going through a breakup, or perhaps it
    was a passage in a
novel.

Some people think of Williamsburg as the "hipster apocalypse"
    and others, the
Orthodox, know the Lord is there with them. She's pushing a
    shopping cart full of plastic
bottles rescued from trash cans.

Crying literally means "to ask for loudly." She mumbles through
    a drop of saltwater, but
She's really saying: You are worthy of asking and having your
    question heard.

Inside, Outside

I see myself as the perpetual outsider.
By living in Queens, I visit the inside –

Manhattan – which was always hopping
with people no matter what time it was.

The streets were alive with the sounds
of introductory remarks. I've met lots

of women at bars and social gatherings.
But few wanted to come home with me.

They said Queens was too far away.
Going to their place was not practical.

The best way to throw
a monkey wrench in the engine before getting

off the ground was to mention going to a hotel.
The conversation would immediately tum

to the topic of bedbugs. They said girls just wanted
to have fun, not search for bedbugs.

I'd rather be an outsider waiting for the milk train.

Alice: Prospect Park, Springtime

But there is also another sense in which seeing comes before words
– John Berger, Ways of Seeing (1972)

Two brown boys climb a magnolia tree
in first flush. Two blackbirds rise
as hymn, or prayer, in praise
of dusk. At times like these,
all the world's a photograph.

fr The Apple

C. T. Louie's as in Egg Store since 'sixties first sale day so nee
port a packing see vee video one fer Naim June, another fer me,
    us two";
draft dodger and four effer time tripping – his magnetic distortions,
closed circuit Buddhadom iconics straight to forty third street
    Jonas' away
Expanded Cinema Festival's TV Bra – Paik exposing Charlotte's
    little tv tubes
over nippled big tits and our trio, me in charge, busted by
    Nu Yuk's badged
finest. Not long behind bars, "bailed out, dismissed."
Later, Paik/Abe's synthesizer @ Gee Bee Aitch Into my
    Rockfellered Teleportraits,
Artists, Babies, Bodies – two-inch professed national public
    brodcasted Unto
2005 – cut to Thea's Berlin werkstadt right, not off, but on her
    wall Paik's words
"When Too Perfect Lieber Gort Wird Sem Bose"
in English – "loving God will be angry" enough said

Blow Bad Blues, Brother Lateef

blow mean bad Blues
with jump and swing
and ev-va-thing!
'Til the 2, 'Til the 4, 'Til the 6AM
sleepy time when the sunrise
sits just over Earth's eyes,
languid on the horizon.

Blow bad Blues Brother Lateef
blow mean bad Blues
the world has never heard before!
Blow to the Four Corners of the Earth
and cover the sky with your horny sax sounds
swingin' with the back-beat Boogie Woogie
of bar room brawls, Big Joe Turner,
and the workin' man drinkin' big to
ease the pain of being stepped on.
Blow of brothel houses,
abusive spouses,
bloody crosses burning
in the heat of the night.
Of blowin' out a tire on the Cadillac,
Flat City halfway to the gig,
on the run and caught
somewhere between nowhere
and nowhere at all.

Blow bad Blues Brother Lateef
blow mean bad Blues
of your hand slidin' up her warm thigh,
makin' love to her
like you make love to your sax!
Sweet Sula momma

snakin' hot tongue
down to your Medulla Oblongata!
Oh baby! Gotta go gotta go I gotta go

Blow bad Blues with Brother Lateef
blow mean bad Blues!
Sing lullabies to the memories
of hot Havana nights.

Drinking wild Cuban Rum
and watching Fidel and Che
takin' back the banks
and kickin' out the Mob.
No mas Traficante for Santo's boys,
and Sweet Sula momma shakin'
her hips not two feet from the band
while Viva La Revolution!
raged just outside the door.
Her cheeks and muscles bulging
with sweat and the sound of gunfire.
The fabric covering her Sweet Sula momma
curves being stretched to impossible tightness,
the shape is where it starts, man!

That's what Brother Lateef says
when he blows bad blues
when he blows mean bad blues
and whispers: It's all in the tellin'.
The sound that paints a picture
is worth a thousand words in the air,
and ten thousand notes on this saxophone.
He whispers this in my ear
then blows a G-Flat
stopping to smile big at me
who is listening to him
blow mean bad blues.

Blow Brother Lateef
blow those Blues
in my ear and out the door
to the streets where
we the people need them.
Where the sidewalks crack under
the weight of the heavy-hearted whose
hope is gone with the slash of a knife.

Send them out with a voice pure enough
to STOP! the fists that pound a woman's
bare white flesh on crowded Sixth Street
and Avenue A as witnesses of all colors
stand by cheering for more.

Lay those Blues down hard to mend the broken of spirit,
the lost and forlorn, tattered and war-torn,
and when you've comforted all of them
turn your Blues to the one who looks
into the mirror and calls himself

me.

Blow bad Blues Brother Lateef
blow mean bad Blues
and I'll meet you out
past the Chicken Shack
with a bottle of wine in my hand,
and my soul intact.
We'll meet and laugh and

Blow bad Blues Brother Lateef,

blow mean bad Blues.

Sleeping with Gregory Corso

I gazelle-leap in two step beats
Your rum and coke breath flies fast and deep
Six flights to Allen's flat
I may need to hug your stocky hand to precipice.
You'd like that.

"Kneel at my feet," you howl, "I will choke you with my charm and
set loose the poem I wrote for your curly locks. Hey! (In fact!)
Let me grab one now as I am slowly slipping off my high horse."
Allen pokes playboy-tail with rolled-up st mark's program.
I yank from above.
We will haul this mad yak to ginzy's temple in record time!

But your shrine hosts newly drawn snapshots –
Sketched mental notes
I can breeze through your mind and other cool places.
sit on your lap while you tell tales of minstrels long ago
Beating time with tongue and drum
Howling truth into ears of the oblivious
The sheets are clean and there is enough rum to drown a shipload
of pirates.

How can I say no to a man
whose twisty antics drive men ditsy
whose unrhymed palaver shoot a gal's knees weak
whose plopped lovebomb rattles poet heaven
whose best and only pick up line is his surname

O Corso I love you!
I want to kiss your clank and eat your thunder
Put a lollipop in your mouth
carve your name
on my bare ass

Corso slept here
track you to Tangiers
Two thumbs out on the highway to poetic passion

Please don't leave me with Orlovsky.
He is weird and his comic books are scary!

Wail for CORSO
For CORSO is dead
Wail for CORSO wail
But what will we do with your bones
and that beautiful tale?

It's November in the South Bronx and Endless Love

is swooping into the apartment windows like an omniscient
narrator, as if it were 1982 all over again, and our bedroom
is the mezzanine tier of Madison Square Garden and Diana
and Lionel are singing solely for our section. It's November

in the South Bronx but winter is still hiding out in a basement
in Hoboken, and Endless Love is pleading with all of Banana
Kelly, promising us a brand of devotion so deep that every
heart becomes a single melody so pristine even the street

sweepers have to stop in their tracks and sigh. It's November.
The elevated subway rails are snapping like faulty toothpicks.
The 3rd Avenue bus is stuffed like a clothing rack at Marshall's.
It's flu season. An unidentifiable stench is punching up through

the sewer grates, and a macho man-child is bludgeoning
Diana's solo with the squeal of his moped, and every corner
is complaining about having to go to work tomorrow, but
something in Lionel's promise to play the fool for Diana

sinks into our socks and seizes us. It's so insipid and earnest
how can you not believe this feeling will last beyond your trip
to the coroner or at least until New Year's? Because some-
times this is what it takes to get you to bed at a sensible hour:

an unreasonable confession made by two bodiless voices
covering Longwood Avenue like pastel linoleum, a middle
school crush convinced no one else will do, a cry of love
drenched in reverb and advertising royalties that when sung

by the neighbors on a warm November night in the South
Bronx can feel like vows being renewed on a fiftieth wedding
anniversary. For even a city this battered and cynical needs
to believe that such maudlin, naïve affection can still conquer

the brick fortresses lining Longwood, a forlorn echo begging
for a hand to hold onto forever plus one. It's November
in the South Bronx and Endless Love is shaking free every
abdicated gym shoe from its sagging telephone wire gallows.

No Yoyo

(he's from New York) ... (from Puerto Rico New York) ...

(he's a new Rican) ... (what they call) ... (a Riqueño) ...

(bein' New) ... (or Trigueño) ... (Speakin' New) ... (or Rican) ...

(a Nuyo seekin' No Yorker) ... (is he New) ... (or a Porter) ...

(a port) ... (of sherry) ... (Cheri Cheri) ...

(Porto Puerto) ... (York, oh) ... (Yoko?) ... (el Coco) ...

(que hablas) ... (se habla Coco?) ... (no'Co) ... (no'City) ...

(port of no'City Rican) ... (a Port o'Ric'er is called) ...

(a bo'Ricuer) ... (a Boricua) ... (a boring'wha?) ... (a bore) ...

(this is boring) ... (into my yawner) ... (what chu saying) ...

(what NEW saying) ... (the new Say) ... (be the new City) ...

(of York) ... (a yorkie) ... (a pit) ... (a bull) ... (a toro) ...

(a To'rres) ... (a No'res) ... (a city nono) ... (a city Yorker, uncorked) ...

(a boozer?) ... (a bozo) ... (a New bozo) ... (yo soy bozo) ...

(in the YO zone, sí) ... (yo soy the NEW Yo) ...

(that's some NEW Yo, bro) ... (yo Rican, sí) ... (soy no Rican) ...

(he's no Rican) ... (from no Ricua) ... (he's no You) ...

(no Yo) ... (no I) ... (the I) ... (in I) ... (is the NEW No) ...

(I be) ... (some a dat) ... (New No) ... (from Noricua, bro)

Carelessly Yours

Lost my footing, carelessly, while rushing to
East Houston Street because your birthday brunch
Demanded smoked brook trout from Russ & Daughters;
Loosened my hold on the handrail of the downtown express
So my fingertips – in search of a passage aligned with
My sentiments for your card or a toast –
Could leaf through a collection of Amichai's love poems,
And stumbled backwards, with a twist,
Grazing a woman who didn't react, and
Coming to a stop with my upper arm pressing against
Someone else's hand gripping a stanchion.
It couldn't have hurt, but his scowl –
As if carelessness is akin to intentionality,
As if he was channeling all the glares
No one else on the train, by convention, would cast,
Despite my sincere apology, with eye contact
(The heartbeat of the human relationship) –
Was that of someone who catalogues all his grievances.

Or, maybe by his glower he was telling me that
Anyone who knows anything about poetry knows
Amichai did not write celebratory love poems,
That his love poems express longing and unsettled regret,
That even when adverting to a lover
His poems atomize time's passage and transient connections;
But they could be a template for the poems we would compose
If we were commanded to love New York City –
Although his poems have nothing to do with New York City –
Because transcendent poems, whatever their intentions,
Like New York City itself; and the universe; and,
The consequences of our carelessness,
Reorient our sensibilities,
Shift the vantage point from which we consider

Dualities and conflicting loyalties and false choices,
The breathtaking vistas of irreducible paradox,
That, without fanfare, configure our essence.

Municipal Cartography

I live in nameless taupe
I realize to my horror
from the map staring at me from the back
of the front seat of the taxi:
below the verdant rectangle labeled Murray Hill,
above the respectable olive of Gramercy Park
and to the right of the solid ochre of Chelsea –
as if 23rd to 34th, Fifth Ave. to the River
were only a conglomeration of arteries
on their way to actual *neighborhoods* –

but it is even worse than I thought,

for as we emerge from the Midtown Tunnel
I see the colors more clearly:
I live in a *gray* area,
not taupe, in fact the identical hue
that covers Brooklyn and Queens,
which seem to have established
a sinister game-board bridgehead
right where I am, Outer Borough invaders
perhaps bivouacking at this very moment
down the block from my building,
in Vincent Albano Park, where a troop
of Clinton and Cornwallis's redcoats
might have also paused for a moment
in September of '76,
in the effort to cut Washington off
from the rest of the Revolution.
To do this they disembarked at Kip's Bay,
supported by a murderous naval cannonade
that scattered the rebel forces, just over there
and back a couple of blocks. So that's where I live:
Kip's Bay. I'll ink it in here on the map
at the next red light.

In the Fisted Hand of May

On Fourteenth Street
The posters throw body parts
Into the pedestrian eye furnace
And I don't walk too close
To the newspaper stands
Or the headlines will bleed
On my shoes. If I encounter
A mud-caked Christ
On the echoing sidewalk
And he laughs like a hyena
When I genuflect
I'll believe in his gospel
Providing he doesn't make hair spray
Of equivalent value
To large tracts of land
But I don't welcome overtures
Or solicitations in public
I acknowledge the doomsday sky
Resembling a bombed city
And the swinging door
That each face throws
Into the emptiness at large

In the amniotic air
My shadow sticks where I pause
I'd opt for a floating forest
Serenaded by an oboe or flute
But it won't happen here
Grounded in pizza smell
And rush hour scream machines
Space is a cage
And the streets are magnetic

New York is a worldly city
But the present is too discrete
If you cling to a past that's too distant
You will never feel part of a crowd
The shirtless beggar who asks for a cigarette
Arouses an obscure double
Carved out of porous stone
Animated by the wind
He fell into this history
I'd give him my social security number
If it would help him to step into time
But numbers are meaningless
To those who are not linear
Lighting his cigarette
He departs into the pink rain
Of a Manhattan sunset
At least that part of him
Which is visible
"Watch out for those vapors"
I caution him
The manholes are ghost traps

The Day Duke Raised: May 24ᵀʰ, 1974

for Duke Ellington

1.

that day began with a shower
of darkness calling lightning rains
home to stone language
of thunderclaps shattering the high
blue elegance of space & time
where a broken-down riderless, horse
with frayed wings
rode a sheer bone sunbeam
road, down into the clouds

2.

spoke wheels of lightning
spun around the hours high up
above those clouds duke wheeled
his chariot of piano keys
his spirit now levitated from flesh
& hovering over the music of most high
spoke to the silence
of a griot-shaman/man
who knew the wisdom of God

3.

at high noon the sun cracked
through the darkness like a rifle shot
grew a beard of clouds on its livid bald
face hung down noon, sky high
pivotal time being a five in the nine
numbers of numerology
as his music was the crossroads
the cosmic mirror of rhythmic gri-gri

4.

so get on up & fly away duke bebop
slant & fade on in strut dance swing riff

float & stroke those tickling gri-gri keys
those satin ladies taking the A train up
to harlem those gri-gri keys of Birmingham
breakdown sophisticated
ladies mood indigo
get on up & strut across gri-gri
raise on up your band's waiting
     5.
thunderclapping music somersaulting
clouds racing across the deep blue wisdom
of God listen it is time for your intro
duke into that other place where the all-time
great band is waiting for your intro duke
it is time for the Sacred Concert, duke
it is time to make the music of God
duke we are listening for your intro

duke let the sacred music begin

Anarchy City

and you will lose again, he says and you will lose again and you will lose you will lose. The anarchy of the city is the anarchy of the heart broken and broke and broken-in on and upon. The anarchy of the city is in anarchy of the lies is the anarchy of unrest of rest of distress and you will lose again, he says and you will lose again and you will lose you will lose

The idleness of manipulation, what is done, and done for, and
                                                         done in.

He can't say; he can't play; he can't delay   anymore.

It's more of the same, and isn't it always the same when fire plays
                                                      with fire?

In anarchy is unrest and in unrest is the reckless, the hopeless, the
                                             fearless, the careless.

In the city of anarchy, in the veil of the city is the first of the city, the caricature of the city, the anxiety of the city is the first of the city, the origin of the city, the knowledge of the city, the beat of the city, the haze of the city, the sketch of the city, the temptation of the city, the menacing of the city, the dismissal of the city, the affluence of the city, the idealism of the city, the scapegoat of the city, the want of the city, the thirst of the city, the horror of the city, the crank of the city, the architect of the city, the people of the city, the people of the anarchy, the anarchy of the people

Listen, this is how it works, anarchy.
We fall in on ourselves.
We fall in on the city,
and the city falls in on us.

And the point is, the struggle is in the disarray; the common good
is in the anarchy An arch

You push back against it by being who you are.

Anarchy is derived from the word *ánarchos*, meaning "without a
head or chief, headless.

Headless.
Even headless,
our city sees
with its eyes.
The disorder
is ordered
without.

Misplaced

Now there's a Target, maybe a Walmart
On Bleecker Street and I rush in, and crash
Into a waitress from my ex-café
I don't remember her, but she remembers me
She's suddenly a tall redhead,
And some other guy who I guess
Was a waiter, and we chat about Bob
Though they keep calling him Roberto
And I recall Bob and his isolation
At the corner of the bar, tucked away
From all the hustle and scuffle, very cool
Possibly the coolest guy I ever met
And he came from Staten Island
So you never know where
The cool dudes will be from

Show You Out the Door

Manhattan's streets I sauntered pond'ring . . .
– Walt Whitman, "Song of Myself"

& I stay alive to look at things
& if I don't look at something beautiful at least once a day –
– go to the Metropolitan – see the Piero with well dressed angels
down from Massachusetts, the
stunning newly-acquired Duccio infant feet symbolically at heart –
I go mad

But the box around the little painting shows your own reflection,
mortifying mirror
where is Virgin compassion (ho hum) in these hungry eyes?

paintings speak . . . traces . . . phonemes . . .
pink (another) on black with gold

Hungry eyes means "someone is looking"
Hungry person like you means you are "not just satisfied"
What is art but some hungry method or let down your voice
in this chamber you supposed to be awed, wholesome
stop complaining about the glass, what these people keep in the
basement, what they are not showing us, museum a theme park

You will never be a rich person looking so strange
pacing the uptown galleries,
the Goya girl seems to follow you with her
eyes, the guard is approaching you
to show you out the door

I wanted to write a walking around poem
beginning with a trip to the Museum, Fifth Avenue was always
wide
was "Zone" influenced by Walt Whitman?

someone asked in Anselm Hollo's lecture class
in the distant school
that went from Apollinaire to Jack Spicer

Could the poets we love exist in one school?

Too passionate about art, poetry, modernism
You were young in it and you were walking the same streets
remember?

before you migrated . . .

Remember the girl couple – remember their embrace
One with dark hair, very tall, deep red fingernails
the other a gamin, pixie
"motion" perspective" "random"
girl as "butch" as "femme" out in the world
too . . . passionate about art, she said, sizing the other one (me) up

&

a fussy curator back inside (we were off the streets now)
said, we were to be looking at the figure as if
from below okay we will try that & stay alive to try that
looking at her holiness as if from below, on my knees if you will
I want to touch it, her, art yes & you could be Walt Whitman
or Gertrude Stein anywhere in this town, revolving doors

Some of the thinking in here includes a metaphor of wolves,
hungry people,
the incarcerated, schools closing, sweet sense of being able to
turn a corner may be fallacious may be true

Turn

& I stay sensate to be loved & love you too & want to drag you

to the heavenly
galleries where my civilization's artifact is free
you can just pay a nickel if you are a citizen
I will pay taxes to support this art but not war
(looking into that)

& love you freely & give you wide love that you could
travel anywhere in this love wide as it goes and it does to these
steps
which take you away from the demonstrations about an illegal war
you come inside & find some shelter here looking at things

& I started – me, an organizer, in love with poetry
– a school far from here
to consider "poetry as thinking" and it was
"best" and it was lineage – O'Hara Chair for a Poet of Deep
Gossip and how we
might look at things amusedly, tragically and talk about "lineage,"
"keep the world safe for poetry" etc.
& an Israeli chair to be occupied by a Palestinian
& a Greek chair to be occupied by a Turk
& Robert Duncan spoke at length that we could intuit reality
& we named a building "Allen Ginsberg" and wept and held
memorials
when a poet dies, reading something aloud, holding books
with hands across the Rockies

& translation of these mental states
& this seems long ago . . . steps . . . founding a school . . .
archival glee . . . when we walked to the Museum
I couldn't get by without seeing something beautiful today
How many millions for a Duccio?
(worth it, she said)
& of course all the poets love a Piero
inestimable pleasure in a Piero

& consider the business of taxes it's soon April
& consider the business of welfare how sad it goes
& consider the business of the end of nature
& the beginning & end of cities & Noam Chomsky
says we'll have suicide bombings soon on home turf
"Have you outstript the rest? Art you the President"
said Walt Whitman

How they are laughing at us in Europe
Europe that we put it in our Museums
How can we be a walking academy of trees
when we are tearing them down?

Walking on Tenth Street

we are walking on tenth street in the direction of neptune a polish diner which simon likes to go to but you have to get there before 11 am if you want the breakfast special and that's important because simon likes to arrive while they're still offering brunch which means unlimited orange juice and endless hot cups of coffee when we run into max camber but no time to stop and talk and besides simon doesn't like max camber these days and he doesn't want to talk to max camber because even though max studied film at ucla he still doesn't know how to approach his subjects with what simon likes to call sympathetic objectivity

and so we shake max's hand and keep on walking and eventually we get to avenue a where the korean green grocer is warming his hands over a chestnut fire and a light rain is coming down and simon tells me about his recent visit to provincetown where he is editing the selected works of robert creeley and how good it is to work with creeley's son because the man's devotion to his father is admirable complete and entirely sincere

and it is spring in the city and the tourists are returning not unlike the last time i came to town to visit simon but that was a different scene we were on our way to drink red wine and listen to jazz at mo pitkin's and we were both of us looking sharp and photogenic and carefree on avenue a when some protestors started to crank things up –

crazy! said simon and it was crazy

it was crazy and colorful and gay it was a parade of angry flowers it was the rosebowl parade & thanksgiving and st patties and maybe even christmas in july and we stopped to watch them and shout things out and smile at them with their big angry banners and their coterie of cops but like i say that was a while ago and we were angels of the new york city night whereas this is a thursday morning in spring and when we get to the diner 'it is already past half eleven" says the waitress in her polite but sad polish accent over the bustling sound of waitresses counter help busboys dishwashers spoons plates and customers

the joyful crash and clink of the world and we looked at the clock on the wall and each other in our ragged clothes and we looked at her and the entire western world working for a living except us

and we don't care anymore

we are happy now
we have found each other
and we don't even mind paying full fare
for our eggs over easy, rye toast

125Th Street

Once there was a Harlem of the mind,
In a New York of green youth and mystery,
Steaming manholes, fevered sleep,
When I was a pilgrim without ambition.

Characters with metal teeth and top hats,
Snake oil and paste-diamond salesmen,
Broadside hawkers from a mythic left,
Selling long dismissed socialist solutions.

Cartoons and old watch shops lined every street.
Bearded purveyors of old country arcana
Beaconed from the storefronts. Craftsmen,
Contrived the shadows they hid in before their attack.

Now I have come to Harlem again – Lexington
And 1-2-5 – so many years later, and not for adventure.
I visit the institutional bland brick building looming
Across from the 2-Brothers pizza shop.

It looks like prison, or asylum from another century,
When you could hear the screams of the residents
In the street. Their pain carried far,
Even muffled by the heavy metal doors.

I sign in, then ride the elevator to the 2nd floor:
Rehab for victims of varied tragedy and disease.
There's some crazy hope given here of returning
To a normal life. The visitors buy into it.

And I've been such a visitor for so long,
The wheelchair-bound residents who line the halls
Calling silently for attention, begging for their meds –
They know my name now, and whom I visit:

How is she? Old Charlie asks everyday,
Rolling down the hall. He's always in good
If medicated spirits, and seems sincere in his question.
She's fine, I say, knowing she's not.

I have no words to keep a conversation going.
I walk up to # 211 – I could find it in my sleep.
That oil brown door was so overwhelming.
My knock is soft, but she knows I'm coming in.

She's grown so thin she can no longer walk,
And does not participate in 2nd floor society.
She keeps her door closed – the only patient who does.
And, having shut out the world, she wastes,

Watches TV in the darkness,
Knowing she will never leave this room.

my sister magdelena was engaged to be married to guiseppe

my sister magdelena was engaged to be married to guiseppe,
place and promised to carry her away from the long days of
toil sewing for pennies from her padrone, and the fire started
like a whisper, hesitantly, like it was pausing in a corner
before it looked into the face of god, then it caught on a waistband,
and a moan rose from each floor, and the fire traveled like it was
burning through paper, because pounds of fabric burn easily,
creating a cauldron of screams and rips and tears, searing through
skin like it was made of cotton, like it was flimsy, and one narrow
window led to a staircase that fell under the weight of panic,
and the elevator cables snapped when someone slid down them,
and the firemen's ladder reached only the sixth floor, many died
without moving, their skin seared to the bone, and someone sat
at the window's edge kissing the star of david or crossing
     themselves
and saying a prayer to jesus to save them before jumping to the
pavement, and magdelena was caught in the backlash of a curl
of fire, closing her mouth with one finger, instructing her to be quiet,
to lay down, till she was ashen, till she floated through the charred
air of lower broadway, drifting toward the east river, like a black
cloud in the late winter sky.

Fishing the East River off the Night Shift, August, 1994

So my line's in the East River and not on the page: twelve pound test, with a diamond jig attached. My name is emblazoned on my work shirt: Joe, in bright yellow letters (as if the supervisors doubt either they or I can remember it). I'm Joe in yellow and laughing with my friend Wally Cruz from rough inspection while the sea gulls dip and dive and a car's bass shakes the concrete slabs that we are risking our bones on. We came here straight from the 12 to 8. Came when the tide was going out. We've run out of squid. We've run out of beer. We haven't caught anything but snags. It's 2 in the afternoon and hot and I'm nodding between casts. I hear Joe! emanating from the bike/jogging path. I ignore it (My name is everywhere, seldom at me, and rhymes with yo). Then I hear: Joe Weil!! and turn. It's a poet from the Knitting Factory I almost dated; except I didn't know that Earl Grey was a type of tea. This gave her pause. Who could blame her? Now she is poised on her bike above me, lit by the high sun, her hair falling in dark ringlets from her helmet. I've seen this movie before: the Fountainhead? Not a bike, but a horse rearing up. Am I Gary Cooper or Patricia Neal? What are you doing? She shouts. I have a surf rod in my hand. I would never think her question as dumb as my ignorance of Earl Grey. I'm fishing. A bead of sweat rolls into my eyeball. Do you eat those fish? She sounds stunned No. I catch and release (I'm lying). She is even more stunned. So you hook the poor things and then throw them back? I start up the rocks to stand even with her, diamond jig dangling. When I am almost at her level, the hook catches in the rock pile, and pulls me backward. I twist to avoid landing on my head, and fall on my hands, scuffing them against the rocks, sustaining a deep gash on my left palm. I am bleeding. A lot. She rides away, leaving me kneeling there, caught by my own diamond jig. Wally shouts up Who was that? I say: A poet I know. He says: You ought to quit knowing poets, buddy. They're bad for your health.

Blue Banshee

she said she's a Banshee
in her tie-dyed dancing sheet
flavored with salt and cockles
she said it's her favorite muumuu
water-spouting hula hoopin'
acorns breakin' me
at the feet stompin' out
the cherries loadin' up
the grapes peach-snapped off
with wine water weight
she's off with her head tossin'
her hair that of Miss Merrimack
with skin most black all down
her back breakin' men
with moves of rubber bullets
on the shard-like grass blessing
silver liquid tins while kickin'
in empty beer mugs at the Shih Tzu
barkin' at the Shaman drummers
Banshee screams
put down your automatics
put down your automatics
Banshee screens the Union Square
as if she's troubled as if she's
a dreamer on the make she said
Go 'head like David Amram
binge flutter tongue scattin' fluster
wag that dog wag the laurel you can't
pull off my Bahamas, mama.
She's said she was losin' herself
while loosening themselves smashin'
against the world not as snapperlicious
nor as band-aid kitsch but in protest,

she said we gotta protest & protect
on how to aid others' needs
her needs them needs
raidin' through our vanity
Banshee said she's untired
like off a high-rise no longer
wondering why the police
can't touch her won't Ziploc
this barricade because
she has set them in a trance
dancin' her Banshee dance

The Moon Takes the E Train

Stumbles drunk from a downtown dive, swirling himself *milkintocoffee* down the stairs and onto the train and then forgets his way home, gets off instead at Forty-Deuce, looks around and remembers the old-style scene, hookers and pornflix, how often in his fullness he would push some poor sucker into *Mr. Nasty's* peepshow, watch him skulk out later, face wiped off, slither home to *bridgeandtunnel,* lighter twenty bucks, but then the whole place went carnival, wax museums and kiddy theatre, life-sized Elmo and Elsa who will pose with you for a hefty tip, and he's looking around at all the lights blinking into the darkened dark, and that's when a couple approaches the moon and asks to take a selfie, how much it would mean what with the moon being the thing that made them fall in love, and the moon has heard this all before, how he's pulled the tides, and planted romance, but really, he has a long, long night ahead, trying to remember which subway will take him back to the sky, but instead, the moon takes a breath, looks at his reflection in the couple's eyes, nestles in between them and smiles.

Three Poems

Ask Me

The wolf moon goes down like butter
on our pancakes made with bean flour.
Wind axes white blazes on the black,
brackish Hudson. Daily errands arise:

Transcribing the diary of Minerva's owl;
Adding scarred sparks to fire's engine;
Zeroing in on water's flying roots.

This is where I find you, half hidden
in the bull rushes, naked and alone.
Dirty silence pushes us together,
combing honey from our unity as we

inherit a new berth in every breath.

I know a keeper when one comes along.
Miracles are makeable if you ask me.

Classic Madhattan

Use locally sourced rye whiskey.
Today we are using Defiant from upstate.
Play Nina Simone's "Memphis in June."

Pit three Bing cherries and put them
into a chilled tumbler.
Add 2 oz chilled Defiant rye

Add 1/2 oz chilled sweet vermouth

Add 1 oz chilled tart cherry juice
2-3 dashes of Bitters

Today we're using "The Bitter Truth."
Strain over ice. It's an instant classic
like you. Making it up as we go.

It's Manhattan in June.
The fountains titter over their fortunes.

Come on Now

Evening stoops under its sodden shawl.
A siren broods; its caterwaul
snarling over blackened roofs.
Someone's on the run.
Wet tires whisper to Avenue C.
"I'm lost without you," they swear.
I wanted to be a matador
in Manhattan, dancing with horns.
I wanted to be a genie
smoking in your coat of arms.
While you gave the raindrops names,
I made up a little song called

"You'll never be happier
than when I was a string on your harp."

Bushwick Bohemia

Para mi gente...
chequealo...

Bushwick on my mind
quinceañeras at the bodega
with their pretty pink dresses
luscious dark eyes
longing to cut the Valencia cakes
while Mr. Softee lingers
over coco helados *y piragüeros*
fighting for the last dollar
Across the street,
santeros dressed in white
with their collares
buying chickens at the poultry shop
for their next tambor
to be held this Sunday
in someone else's crowded basement
Maggie cruisin' back and forth
 back and forth
keeping the dealers in check
as the sounds of beepers
Rottweiler fights
Freestyle
& chanting from the Pentecostal church
fill the air with the smells
of pernil, alcapurrias y empanadas
from La Claribel –
the best *cuchifrito* in town
Up on the roof,
Miguelito giving blowjobs
to grey-haired old men
so that he can get a fade
at Paul's boutique
or buy mami that fake painting

she wanted for $5.99
down Knickerbocker Avenue
Malitza walking by
pregnant with her second baby
only 18 & already night manager at McDonald's
She wasn't gonna end up consumed
in the empty little crack bags
she counted
every morning
on her way to Grover Cleveland High School
Hector, her boyfriend,
 home from playing handball all day
lying shirtless on the couch blunted out of his mind
staring at the roach on the ceiling
one single roach in a vast desert
or maybe an alien exploring a new world
the ceiling fan –
his spaceship
Doña Carmen sneezing so loud
the walls so thin
Hector says 'Salud'
& she hears him from the second floor
over Walter Mercado
on Canal 41
Turning off the kitchen lights
so that the roaches can scurry into the darkness –
their freedom
like the children playing out all night
Waiting for the L train
 'Mira, Georgie...
Gimme a quarter!'
'Fine...
but cha betta pay me back tomorrow!'
Life in Bushwick,
Ain't it a trip!
One day we'll all be buried
beneath the ground we spit on

First Snow

If I met your eyes across the table,
one passing of a saltshaker
would have made our blood run forever warmer.

Walking through Prospect Park,
I wouldn't wait until the last bench to kiss you.

We would rent a place on the corner of 1st and 1st,
befriend the working poets
who would improvise surrealist ballads
at seeing us stuck on a median, crossing Houston.

We would make impulsive decisions when buying lemons,
make spreadsheets if planning travels,
raise a few children savvy in French baked goods,
or maybe remain alone, just the two of us.

And even if we fell out,
started separate families,
we'd always be at arm's reach,
even across the globe,
even if we went decades without talking.

But here I am, sitting under an oak
in a cemetery in Ridgewood, New Jersey,
while somewhere in Malaysia, or Norway,
two of your ancestors are sharing a Coke.

Rushing out to Whole Foods last night,
I saw your shape on the hood of my pickup truck,
traced in rock-hard snow.

Over my head, the Almighty must have been grinning.

When you look up at the same Almighty,
you won't notice the change in the radius of the Sun.

Like me, you'll wish to know the nature of consciousness,
drink coffee to fall asleep faster.

And maybe one day you'll pick up a metal detector,
hover it over a beach
where I've dropped some good-luck medallion,
dig it up,
and wonder what it is.

Letter to My Friends

It is a good thing my little dog and loyal friend for many years
is dead
because – thanks to the 45th President – I am not alone
no, I am not alone when I say I am afraid to walk around
my beloved city, my beloved angry city
no longer crawling with hombres, yellow cabs, and rent-a-
rickshaws
no longer open to all night movie houses, after hours bars,
    and parking lot flea markets
my beloved angry chewed-up city, my mercurial cerulean
salamander
    city
my city abandoned by the feckless rich and overrun with panting
    beggars
now that I am lucky enough to have been born in a stinking
shithole
and slink about – a sneaky diseased little slanty-eyed fuck

221

At 63 I've started to compost
in La Plaza, a park I helped to save
starting in 1987 and
succeeding in 2002. Some things
take time like a poem you want to write
or onion skins and carrot peels rotting
to loam. A lot gets done in the dark out
of sight. The evidence tells us not to
give up. You have to remember it's not
always fun. Sit down and do it and it
will get done. From my window you could
see the World Trade Center till 9/11.
Another building rises there making
its appearance. My friends, the ends begin

104 Bus Uptown

How bad can it be,
dear wacky New York City,
when the first twelve lines
of "The Love Song of J. Alfred Prufrock"
blink down at me
from a poster on this bus
brought to us
courtesy of the MTA
and the Poetry Society of America
(of which, incredibly, I am a member!)
and, to its right, above the rear door,
another poster: Charles Reznikoff's little poem
about how "the lights go out—"
in the subway
"but are on again in a moment,"
a poem I will be teaching to my students
in a few weeks' time.

Perched in the center back seat
(she got on at Seventh Avenue and 42nd Street),
sitting all alone, as if on a tiny stage
lit by the bus-window daylight of midtown New York,
the attractive actress Beverly D'Angelo
whom I can't bring myself to ask
if she is Beverly D'Angelo, except that I
recognize the perfection of her charming overbite
as she chews gum like mad under wild blue eyes agog,
behaving as if she's never sat on a bus before
or as if she expects a passenger to leap up
at any moment and cry, "Action!,"
with the cameras rolling like the eyes in my head
as I turn now and again to look at her
in her white jacket and skirt that don't

quite match, a silk turquoise blouse
that color-keys her enormous eyes

(which just got off with the rest of her
at 57th and Eighth), and I'm lucky enough
to have been handed this piece of paper
twenty minutes ago
by someone on the street who must be
a secret agent for poetry, though it seems
to be merely an advertisement flyer
for 45th Street Photo, on the back of which
I've just written this poem

Three New Yorkers

Annie Lanzillotto

took as her metaphor the Spaldeen, the New York City ball.
Spaldeens, she wrote, took on the smell of the street. Spaldeens
sweated and got dirty.
Spaldeens taught her soul to find adventure, to fly, to roll, to hide,
to float, to be buoyant –
    and to bounce back.

Annie! Immunocompromised, quarantined, hospitalized
with double pneumonia, a deflated immune system, and recurring
tumors through the years
from Hodgkin's lymphoma at 18, thyroid cancer at 37,
Sole survivor of a group at Brown who called themselves Terminal
Teens.
Emblem of fragility, just this side of poverty, mortality in her
bones.
In her mind's eye, the harder you hit the pavement, the higher
you fly

all the way to St. Raymond & Zerega in the Bronx
where we play an eternal game of catch
on the block where her Bronx accent comforts the dying and the
sick.
And when her ailing, damaged world rolls down the drain by
the gutter.
I hold her feet, lower her in.
She reaches out with her humor, peers with insight,
plucks meaning from the gutter like a lost Spaldeen.

Joe Gould

Raising his glass, Joe Gould proclaimed
I suffer from delusions of grandeur!
I believe myself to be Joe Gould.

Trading stories for drinks
the 1950s eccentric set out to write an
Oral History of Our Time,

I could see the whole thing in my mind,
bushwa, gab, palaver, hogwash, flapdoodle, and malarkey,

he mused, as he poured ketchup on an empty plate
under his portrait at the Minetta Tavern.
Ketchup! The world's only free food!
But no one has ever seen that manuscript, Mr. Gould.

I'm writing primarily for my own amusement – totally unschooled –
Because, well, I happen to be the only Joe Gould in this solar system –
Though there are probably other systems full of Joe Goulds –
a possibility I don't wish to exclude.

Dick Zigun

Yale Playwright who defined Honky Tonk as the opposite of
Hoity Toity.
then bought a building on the Coney Island Boardwalk
stood by Sideshows by the Seashore in an antique bathing suit
ballying Otis the Frog Boy till it closed at 10:30.

And when Kathryn told him, I love that place
he said, *I am that place.*

And he *was* that place for 50 years.
Now, everything is going franchise, he says, *everything's disappearing—*
The loss is the loss — of a certain type of person —
because it's no longer seen as a noble pursuit to run a place that's quirky.

I'm blessed to be the freak flag for a whole liberating energy —
for the 50,000 people who think the Mermaid Parade is cool,
going topless with tits that sag.

I defend the right to be tattooed on your face or have a pierced tongue,
even though you're a teenage suburban girl from Long Island.
Someone's got to carry the flag, declare this freak show worthy.

   — based on an interview with Dick Zigun by Kathryn Adisman

"NY Trilogy: Adam and Eve" by Steve Dalachinsky

Authors' Bios

Dr. Grisel Y. Acosta became a professional poet in New York City by meeting her heroes in Harlem and the Lower East Side, starting in 1999. She is patiently awaiting the moment when music venues and bookstores dominate the landscape again. She is a full professor at the City University of New York-BCC. Her first book of poetry, *Things to Pack on the Way to Everywhere*, is an Andrés Montoya Poetry Prize 2020 finalist and available from Get Fresh Books. Other select work can be found in *Best American Poetry, The Baffler, Red Fez, Gathering of the Tribes Magazine, Paterson Literary Review*, and *Celebrating Twenty Years of Black Girlhood: The Lauryn Hill Reader*. A Geraldine Dodge Foundation Poet, Macondo Fellow, and editor of *Latina Outsiders Remaking Latina Identity*. Her work focuses on her Colombian/Cuban immigrant parents, Afro-Latinx and indigenous ancestry, queer identity, the punk and house music subcultures, and the destruction of postcolonial neoliberalism in educational environments.

Kim Addonizio is the author of a dozen books of poetry and prose, most recently the poetry collection *Now We're Getting Somewhere* (W.W. Norton) and the memoir *Bukowski in a Sundress* (Penguin). Her work has been translated into several languages including Arabic, Catalan, Chinese, Hebrew, Italian, and Spanish. Her Italian grandparents immigrated to New York City around the turn of the previous century, and her father, one of their nine children, was born and raised there. She lived in the city from 2013-2016, subletting near Union Square, in the Bowery, on Avenue C, and in Williamsburg. She is planning to return to New York in 2022, and can be found online at https://www.kimaddonizio.com.

Carlos Aguasaco, a New Yorker by choice, is one of the central figures of the new Hispanic American Poetry in the US. He is Professor of Latin American Cultural Studies and Chair in the Department of Interdisciplinary Arts and Sciences of City College of the City University of New York. He has edited eleven literary anthologies and published seven books of poems, most recently *The New York City Subway Poems* (Ashland Poetry Press, 2020). Carlos directs The Americas Poetry Festival of New York and coordinates The Americas Film Festival of New York. He has traveled extensively to Europe, Asia, Africa, and the

Americas, yet is always happy to return to New York and to read and write poems while commuting in the subway between Queens and Manhattan.

Sandra Alcosser founded SDSU's MFA program and edits *Poetry International*. Her poems have appeared in *The New Yorker, The New York Times, Paris Review, Ploughshares, Poetry* and the *Pushcart Prize Anthology*. She received two individual artist fellowships from National Endowment for the Arts, and her books of poetry, *A Fish to Feed All Hunger and Except by Nature*, received the highest honors from National Poetry Series, Academy of American Poets and Associated Writing Programs, as well as the Larry Levis Award and the William Stafford Award for Poetry.. She was the National Endowment for the Arts' first Conservation Poet for the Wildlife Conservation Society and Poets House in NYC. Like Sylvia Plath, Joan Didion, Sandra Gilbert, Grace Schulman, Heather Mc Hugh and other women writers, Sandra Alcosser flew to NYC as a *Mademoiselle* Guest Editor in Fiction and Poetry her senior year in college, and she stayed.

Carol Alexander says "If I had grown up between the Hudson and the East River, maybe I wouldn't have had to look up the number of bridges that lead in and out of Manhattan (21)." After half a lifetime in New York City, Alexander continues to be intrigued and bemused by the constructed environment where seagulls always seem to be laughing at human endeavor. "Lacking a good sense of direction, I frequently discover unfamiliar corners of the city, yet rarely recall which subway stop they're closest to." Her most recent book is *Fever and Bone*, a collection of poems that mourns our collective loss and anticipates the city's renascence.

Austin Alexis is a native New Yorker. "I have visited many places in the USA, Europe and Canada, but never lived outside of New York City. I've worked in four out of the five boroughs of NYC (and also in Nassau County), but slept in Brooklyn and Manhattan only." His full-length poetry collection is *Privacy Issues* (Broadside Lotus Press, Detroit, Naomi Long Madgett Poetry Award), and his two chapbooks are from Poets Wear Prada (Hoboken, NJ). His chapbook *Lovers and Drag Queens* was a Small Press Review (California) Pick of the Month.

Miguel Algarín (1941-2020) was a Nuyorican poet, writer, co-founder of the Nuyorican Poets Cafe, and a Rutgers University professor. Born in Puerto Rico in 1941, he emigrated to the Lower East Side of NYC with his family in 1950. After pursuing graduate studies in literature in several US universities he returned to Manhattan, and his apartment became a mecca for poets in 1975. Along with Miguel Piñero, Pedro Pietri and others, in the 1980s he founded the Nuyorican Poets Cafe, one of the key cultural institutions of the Nuyorican movement, and a location fo popularization of slam poetry. Algarín played an important role in the spread of Nuyorican literature by compiling, with Miguel Piñero, its first anthology *Nuyorican Poetry: An Anthology of Puerto Rican Words and Feelings,* launching Arte Public Press, which became a leading publishing house for Nuyorican works, and *Aloud: Voices from the Nuyorican Poets Café* (1994) which he co-edited with Bob Holman. Algarín's books include *Mongo Affair, On Call* (1980), *Body Bee Calling from the 21st Century* (1982), *Time's Now/Ya es tiempo* (1985), and *Love Is Hard Work: Memorias de Loisaida/Poems* (1997, Lower East Side Memories/Poems). He received three American Book Awards and became the first Latino to win the Before Columbus Lifetime Achievement American Book Award in 2009.

Hala Alyan is a Palestinian American writer and clinical psychologist whose work has appeared in The New York Times, Poetry, Guernica and elsewhere. Her poetry collections have won the Arab American Book Award and the Crab Orchard Series. Her debut novel, *Salt Houses,* was published by Houghton Mifflin Harcourt in 2017, and was the winner of the Arab American Book Award and the Dayton Literary Peace Prize. Her second novel, *The Arsonists' City,* was recently published by Houghton Mifflin Harcourt. "I live in Brooklyn with my husband and dog and I'm still mourning the closure of Cornelia Street Cafe and Angelica Kitchen."

E.J. Antonio was born and raised in East and Central Harlem and the South Bronx, and her work reflects the rhythms of life in NYC. She has received fellowships in Poetry from the New York Foundation for the Arts, the Hurston/Wright Foundation, and the Cave Canem Foundation. She is the author of two chapbooks, *Every Child Knows*; Premier Poets Chapbook Series 2007 and *Solstice,* Red Glass Books, 2013, a jazzoetry cd, *Rituals in the marrow: Recipe for a jam session.* She is a founding member of the Jazz & Poetry Choir Collective, which released its debut cd *We Were Here,* in the spring of 2020, and a founding board member of the non-profit Arts organization, One Breath Rising.

Dorothy Friedman August is a widely published award winning poet who has won two New York Foundation of the Arts fellowship and won an Acker Award in Poetry for writing and activism. A downtown New York activist, writer and editor for over forty years, she's published three books of poetry and in numerous periodicals and anthologies, and was poetry editor of *Downtown* Magazine from 1984-1996, during the heyday of the East Village zeitgeist when the area was bristling with clubs, galleries, experimentation and street art. She coordinated readings for The Living Theater on East 3rd Street, featuring Allen Ginsberg, Herbert Huncke, Taylor Mead and others, and protested the ousting of the homeless and closing of Tompkins Square Park in 1988 along with artists and squatters. Currently she's writing a memoir, *The Bastard Heirs*, about her life on the lower east side and two poetry collections: *The L Shaped Room*, to be published by Poets Wear Prada, and *Drinking Alaska*, a romp through postmodernism.

Peter Balakian's first job was an office boy and mail runner in the late '60s for Pittston Stevedoring Company on 17 Battery Place. He trained for football running through the back alleys and side streets of lower Manhattan and knew most of the unnamed hamburger joints along the way. His books include *Ozone Journal*, which won the 2016 Pulitzer Prize for poetry and *Black Dog of Fate*, which won the PEN/Albrand Award for memoir. His forthcoming book of poems, *No Sign*, will be published by the University of Chicago Press. He teaches at Colgate University.

Ellen Bass's most recent books are *Indigo, Like a Beggar*, and *The Human Line*. (Copper Canyon Press, 2020, 2014, & 2007). She is also coauthor of *The Courage to Heal: A Guide for Women Survivors of Child Sexual Abuse* (HarperCollins, 1988). Among her honors are Fellowships from the Guggenheim Foundation, the NEA and the California Arts Council, The Lambda Literary Award, and three Pushcart Prizes. She teaches in Pacific University's MFA program and is a Chancellor of the Academy of American Poets. "New York, and specifically, Florence Howe's Upper West Side apartment, has been my home away from home for many years. Florence Howe was my mentor, beginning back in the 1960s at Goucher College and opened the world of poetry to me."

Charles Bernstein is the recipient of the 2019 Bollingen Prize. An ethnic Upper West Sider (riding on the A, B, C & 1, 2, 3), he moved to Brooklyn in 2013, right on the F and G lines. "Alphabet of the Tracks" is from his most recent collection, *Topsy-Turvy* from the University of Chicago Press (2021). Chicago has also recently published *Near/Miss* and *Pitch of Poetry*.

Anselm Berrigan's kids play in NYC parks that were too gnarly to play in when he was a kid. He's experienced blackouts, hurricanes, terrorist attacks, drunk cab drivers driving away with his bags, muggings turning into deep philosophical conversations, angry dogs and punks, riots on his block, evictions, fires, and long bike rides through an emptied pandemic-stricken city. He's the author of a number of poetry books, most recently *Pregrets*, from Black Square Editions, and works mostly as a teacher and editor. From 1998-2007 he worked in various capacities at The Poetry Project at St. Mark's Church, including four years as its Artistic Director.

Luciann Two Feathers Berrios is a published poet, tarot reader, custom crystal healing jewelry maker born and raised in Astoria, New York. She has been a voice for female empowerment through her written publications such as *Women of Eve's Garden: an Anthology*, a poetry collection she curated, edited, and contributed to, consisting solely of female and non-binary voices. She is currently partnering with a nonprofit in Puerto Rico, Women in Need PR, on a soon to be released collection of women's stories on surviving abuse. She has a BA in English Language Arts from Hunter College and an MA in Journalism and New Media from Griffith College in Ireland.

Ama Birch is the author of *Faces in the Clouds, Sonnet Boom!, Ferguson Interview Project* and a video game available for Android, "Space Quake by Ama Birch." She has a Master of Fine Arts in Creative Writing from the California Institute of the Arts and a Bachelor of Arts in Theatre Arts from the State University of New York at New Paltz. She was born on the Lower East Side during a blizzard.

Star Black arrived in New York City in 1977 as a photographer for United Press International. She went freelance in 1980, photographing for *The New York Times*, the Museum of Modern Art and other clients while studying poetry at Brooklyn College with John Ashbery and earning an MFA degree in 1984. She is the author of seven books of poems, the most recent being *The Popular Vote* that addresses the aftermath of the 2016 presidential election. Her collages have been exhibited at Poets House and The Center for Book Arts. She co-founded the KGB Bar Monday Night Poetry Series in the East Village in 1997, which continues today, and has taught poetry at The New School and at Stony Brook University.

Max Blagg is English-born and has lived in New York City since 1972. He has performed at numerous NYC venues including The Kitchen, Guggenheim Museum, Jackie 60, St Marks Church, The National Arts Club, CBGB's and Tin Pan Alley Bar. His most recent publications are *Walkabout NYC* and *Slow Dazzle*, both published by Shallow Books NYC, and just arrived is a collaboration with artist Curtis Kulig, *Loud Money*, a mashup of art and text encased in a splendid hardcover book (Paradigm Publishing). Blagg has collaborated with many artists including Jamie Nares, Alex Katz, Jack Pierson, Richard Prince, Lucy Winton, Keith Sonnier, Nan Goldin, Jerelyn Hanrahan and Nicholas Rule, and is currently collaborating with sound artist DJ IZM on a new audio/visual project.

Jennifer Blowdryer, nee Jennifer Baring-Gould Megan Waters, wrote these *American Haiku* while loitering endlessly in Hells Kitchen, listening. She has a few books out that circulate on Alibris, ABE, and (shudder) Amazon. Currently, she's writing and recording songs with Ace musicians, lives in the East Village, and spends time in Kips Bay, 25th St and 3rd Ave, NYC.

Robert Bly (1926-2021) was one of the most celebrated poets of our time. His *Collected Poems* are published by W. W. Norton. As a young man, he spent three apprentice years in New York, living "in tiny rooms – the better ones had a hot plate – ...determined to write twelve hours a day at least six days a week.... I sometimes didn't talk for a week."

Meagan Brothers writes novels for young adults, the most recent of which, *Weird Girl and What's His Name*, was named one of Kirkus Review's Best Teen Books of 2015. Her poetry has appeared in *POSTblank Magazine* and *Maintenant*, as well as the anthologies *Persian Sugar in English Tea, Before Passing,* and *The Other Side of Violet*. A native Carolinian, she currently lives in New York City, where she buys music at Academy Records, groceries at Fairway, coffee from the Sensuous Bean, and pizza at Big Nick's.

Joseph Bruchac lives in the Adirondack mountain foothills town of Greenfield Center, New York, in the same house where his maternal grandparents raised him. Much of his writing draws on that land and his Native American ancestry. With his late wife, Carol, he founded the Greenfield Review Literary Center and The Greenfield Review Press. He has edited a number of anthologies of contemporary poetry and fiction, including *Songs from this Earth on Turtle's Back, Breaking Silence* (winner of an American Book Award) and he has authored more than 120 books for adults and children, Dr. Bruchac has past residence in NYC as a visiting American studies scholar at Columbia University, and was engaged by the National Museum of the American Indian-New York to write the text on the permanent outside exhibit tables telling the story of the museum and Manhattan's indigenous past.

Regie Cabico won the Nuyorican Poets Cafe Grand Slam and received the Barnes and Noble Writers for Writers Award for his work teaching young adults at Bellevue Hospital. He received his BFA from NYU Tisch School of the Arts and has lived in the West Village, East Village & Williamsburg, Brooklyn. He resides in Washington, DC where he produces and publishes poetry with Capfire Spoken Word Arts.

Steve Cannon (1935-2019) was one of 13 children, born in New Orleans, Louisiana in 1935. He moved to New York City in 1962 after receiving his PhD in World History from the London School of Economics. Steve served as a Professor of the Humanities at Medgar Evers College for many years. Poet, playwright and novelist, he was the author of the underground sensation *Groove, Band and Jive Around*, published by Olympia Press, in 1969. He founded *A Gathering of the Tribes* in 1991, at first as a literary magazine documenting the vibrant culture and work of contemporary artists and writers of the Lower East Side. By 1993 Tribes quickly grew into a salon, art gallery, small press and performance space which he ran for nearly 30 years from his three story-brownstone home on Avenue C and East 3rd Street.

Peter Carlaftes was born in the Bronx and lives in the Village. He has published two books of poetry – *Drunkyard Dog* and *I Fold With Hand I was Dealt*; two collections of his plays – *Triumph for Rent* and *Teatrophy*; and he edits the annual dada journal, *Maintenant*. He is co-director of Three Rooms Press.

Dr. Melissa Castillo is Assistant Professor of English at Lehman College in the Bronx, specializing in Latinx Literature and Culture. She is the author of the poetry collection *Coatlicue Eats the Apple*, editor of the anthology, *¡Manteca!: An Anthology of Afro-Latina Poets*, and co-editor of *La Verdad: An International Dialogue on Hip Hop Latinidades*. Her latest, *A Mexican State of Mind: New York City and the New Borderlands* *of Culture*, examines the creative worlds and cultural productions of Mexican migrants in New York City. An avid marathon runner, Melissa enjoys exploring New York City on her two legs or with her two dogs, Mighty Mouse and Luna.

Neeli Cherkovski is a San Francisco based poet, biographer and essayist with strong personal associations with Charles Bukowski, Bob Kaufman and other major figures in West Coast poetry. Recent publications are *Hang out on the Yangtze River* and *Elegy for My Beat Generation*. A regular visitor to NYC, where his uncle Herman Cherry helped found The Five Spot, he is author of *Whitman's Wild Children* and is currently writing for *The Brooklyn Rail*.

Andy Clausen was born in a bomb shelter in 1943 and raised in East Oakland CA. In 1965 after reading Kerouac and hearing Allen Ginsberg he decided to be a Beat Poet. His poetry books include *Extreme Unction, Shoe-be-do-be-ee-op, Austin Texas Austin Texas, The Iron Curtain of Love, Without Doubt, The Streets of Kashi, Festival of Squares, Trek to the Top of the World, Home of the Blues* and his memoir, *BEAT: The Latter Days of the Beat Generation, a First-Hand Account.* "I lived in NYC a few times in the eighties, nineties, 2000s, taught poetry in the schools for over ten years, and often stayed at Ginsberg's 12th St. apartment and other poet's houses."

Andrei Codrescu's recent poetry book is *No Time Like Now* (Pitt Series, 2019). During pandemic lockdown in Brooklyn, he recorded a 13-part story podcast, *Walls & Curtains*, available on social media, and collaborated with Vincent Katz on a year-long (2021) poem, "An Epic of Care."

Douglas Collura lives in Manhattan and is the author of a spoken-word CD, *The Dare of the Quick World*, and the book, *Things I Can Fit My Whole Head Into*, which was a finalist for the 2007 Paterson Poetry Prize. He was also the 2008 First Prize Winner of the Missouri Review Audio/Video Competition in Poetry. He was nominated for a Pushcart Prize in 2016, 2018 and 2020 and has been published in numerous periodicals.

Brenda Coultas' poetry can be found in *Bomb, Brooklyn Rail*, and the anthology *Readings in Contemporary Poetry* published by the DIA Art Foundation and *Infiltration* from Station Hill Press. *The Tatters*, an elegy to the pigeon feathers and telephone booths of New York City, was published in 2014. Due in 2022 is *The Writing of an Hour*, through

Wesleyan University Press. "I moved to NYC from the Midwest in the mid-90s to work as staff at the Poetry Project."

Lorraine Currelley, poet, spoken word artist, multi-genre writer, Pearls of Wisdom storyteller, curator and multimedia visual artist. Named Bronx Beat Poet Laureate State of New York 2020–2022 by the National Beat Foundation. She has curated exhibits for arts and literary organizations. She's a widely anthologized and a multi-awards recipient. Recognized for her commitment to serving literary, social justice, senior and mental health communities. She's the executive director for both Poets Network & Exchange, Inc. and the Bronx Book Fair. Inc. She's a mental health counselor with certification in Thanatology (grief and bereavement.) She resides in New York City.

Steve Dalachinsky (1946-2019) wrote poetry, haiku, music criticism, CD liner notes, travelogues and had a long running column: *Outtakes* in *The Brooklyn Rail*. Many collaboration CDs with musicians such as Matthew Shipp, Joëlle Léandres and The Snobs. His publications include *The Final Nite: A Complete Notes from a Charles Gayle Notebook 1987-2006* (Ugly Duckling Presse); *Superintendent's Eyes* (Autonomedia); *Reaching Into The Unknown* (RogueArt); *Flying Home* (Paris-Lit-Up); *Fool's Gold* (Feral Press); *Where Night and Day become One* (Great Weather for MEDIA). He received the PEN Oakland National Book Award, the Chevalier de l'Ordre des Arts et Lettres, Acker Award, Kafka Award, and Benjamin Franklin Award. Steve was born and grew up in Brooklyn, and spent most of his adult life in Manhattan, living in a tenement apt. in Soho with his wife, painter and poet, Yuko Otomo.

Toi Derricotte is the recipient of the 2020 Frost Medal from Poetry Society of America. Her sixth collection of poetry, *I: New and Selected Poems*, was published in 2019 and shortlisted for the 2019 National Book Award. Her literary memoir, *The Black Notebooks*, won the Anisfield-Wolf Book Award for Non-Fiction and was a *New York Times* Notable Book of the Year. Her numerous literary awards include fellowships from the Guggenheim Foundation, the Rockefeller Foundation, and the National Endowment for the Arts. "I lived in the New York area and taught in the Poets-in-the-School program for twenty years, taught in hundreds of schools and remember many of my students poems by heart!"

JP DiBlasi is a native New Yorker who, as a child, was taught by her mother to ride New York City's subways - the A uptown to the Cloisters, the E or the F to St. Patrick's Cathedral and the 1 or the 2 to Macy's on 34th Street. JP soon learned any of the first five letters of the alphabet (A, B, C, D, E) would speed her to the Arch in Washington Square Park and to the culture of The Village. She currently lives and writes in the Hudson River town of Ossining, NY, remaining close to the City subways and the memories of Chumley's, Gerde's, and the White Horse Tavern. Her poems have been published in *Never Forgotten: 100 Poets Remember 911* (North Sea Poetry Scene Press), *Carrying The Branch: Poets in Search of Peace* (Glass Lyre Press), *Poetry Breakfast* and *RiverRiver.* Her chapbook, *No Longer Gravity's Partner* (Blue Light Press), was published in 2019.

Diane di Prima (1934-2020) began writing as a child and by the age of 19, was corresponding with Ezra Pound and Kenneth Patchen. Her first book of poetry, *This Kind of Bird Flies Backward*, was published in 1958 by Hettie Jones and LeRoi Jones' Totem Press. Born in Brooklyn, she attended Hunter College High School and Swarthmore College before dropping out to be a poet in Manhattan, where she edited the newspaper *The Floating Bear* with Amiri Baraka (LeRoi Jones) and was co-founder of the New York Poets Theatre. She spent time in California at Topanga Canyon, returned to New York City, and eventually moved to San Francisco permanently, where she was a Poet Laureate. Di Prima was known for her activism, having been exposed early on to political consciousness by her grandfather, Domenico, as detailed in her memoir *Recollections of My Life as a Woman*. Her book *Revolutionary Letters* (rereleased in 2021 in its 50th anniversary expanded edition by City Lights) cemented her position as a committed political advocate among the Beats.

Margarita Drago, originally from Argentina, was denied the right to live in her country and came to the United States as a political refugee after five years of captivity during the last Argentinean dictatorship. In 1981 she moved to New York City. "In NY I made my professional career, became a published author, and met extraordinary people, especially women writers, artists and freedom fighters. The skyscrapers, the lights, the people, are all part of my poetic imagery." Author of *Fragmentos de la Memoria / Memory Tracks, Fragments from Prison (1975-1980)* she has co-authored a book of women testimonies, *Tomamos la Palabra: Mujeres en la Guerra Civil de El Salvador (1980-1992).* As an ex-political prisoner, poet, writer and college professor at the City University of New York, she has represented Argentina in congresses, poetry festivals and book fairs in the US, several Latin American countries, Canada, Spain, and France.

Denise Duhamel lived in New York City from 1985 to 1999 – and these were the happiest, most exciting years of her life. Her most recent book of poetry is *Second Story* (Pittsburgh, 2021). Her other titles include *Scald; Blowout; Ka-Ching!; Two and Two; Queen for a Day: Selected and New Poems; The Star-Spangled Banner;* and *Kinky.* A recipient of fellowships from the Guggenheim Foundation and the National Endowment for the Arts, Duhamel teaches in the MFA program at Florida International University in Miami. "My mother tells a story that in 1966, when I was five, our family took a trip to New York City. We went to the Statue of Liberty, the Empire State Building, and Central Park. It was while walking in Times Square past overflowing trashcans and strip joints, I turned to my parents and little sister and said, '"When I grow up I am going to be a writer and live here.'"

Cornelius Eady is a poet, playwright and singer, songwriter whose poetry collections include: *Victims of the Latest Dance Craze*, winner of the 1985 Lamont Prize; *The Gathering of My Name*, nominated for a 1992 Pulitzer Prize; *Brutal Imagination* (a finalist for the 2001 National Book Award, and a recent addition to Kindle), and *Hardheaded Weather*. Though his teaching and reading gigs take him far, all roads lead him back to the West Village. He currently splits his time between Manhattan and Knoxville, where he teaches at the Univ. of Tenn., (where he holds the Hodges Chair), and is co-founder of the Cave Canem Foundation.

Tongo Eisen-Martin is San Francisco Poet Laureate, author of *Heaven is all Goodbyes* (City Lights, 2017), and recipient of the California Book Award for Poetry, an American Book Award, and a PEN Oakland Book Award. "New York, in some ways, is my first home for poetry. When I went there to college, I made my way down to the Nuyorican Cafe almost the first day. It was like a youngster stepping into Minton's playhouse, where the samurai are getting busy."

David M. Elsasser has been active in the New York City poetry scene since the 1990s. He is a board member of the West Side Arts Coalition, on the Upper West Side of Manhattan, where he runs poetry readings in a one-time subway station, on the Broadway median. He co-hosted the long-running Saturn Series Poetry Reading in the East Village, from 2002 to 2011, and runs a peer poetry workshop, The Parkside Poets, from his apartment overlooking Central Park. His first poetry chapbook, *Last Call*, was published by Poets Wear Prada, and his second, *Delicious*, was published by NoNet Press, a label he launched with other Parkside Poets.

Elaine Equi moved from Chicago to New York with her husband, poet Jerome Sala, in 1988. They took up residence on Mulberry Street (still her favorite street in the city). She remembers seeing Martin Scorsese in the neighborhood – and him saying, "Yes, it's me." Equi's most recent book is *The Intangibles* from Coffee House Press. Her other books include *Voice-Over*, which won the San Francisco State Poetry Award; *Ripple Effect: New & Selected Poems*, which was a finalist for the *L.A. Times* Book Award and on the short list for The Griffin Poetry Prize; and *Sentences and Rain*. She teaches in the MFA Program in Creative Writing at The New School.

Martín Espada was born in the East New York section of Brooklyn in 1957. He has published more than twenty books as a poet, editor, essayist and translator. His latest book of poems is called *Floaters* (2021, winner of the National Book Award). Other collections of poems include *Vivas to Those Who Have Failed* (2016), *The Trouble Ball* (2011), and *Alabanza* (2003). He is the editor of *What Saves Us: Poems of Empathy and Outrage in the Age of Trump* (2019). His honors include the Ruth Lilly Poetry Prize, the Shelley Memorial Award, and a Guggenheim Fellowship. A former tenant lawyer, Espada is a professor of English at the University of Massachusetts-Amherst.

Gil Fagiani (1945-2018) was an independent scholar, translator, essayist, short-story writer, and poet who wrote nine books of poetry including his Connecticut trilogy, *Chianti in Connecticut, Stone Walls, Missing Madonnas, Rooks, A Blanquito in El Barrio, LOGOS*, the soon-to-be published bilingual collection, *Looking for an Echo* and two chapbooks, *Grandpa's Wine* and *Serfs of Psychiatry*. He spent his early years in the Villa Avenue section of the Bronx. His parents moved to Stamford, Connecticut and Fagiani returned to East Harlem during his young adulthood where he experienced a political transformation. He referred to the Bronx and East Harlem as his muses. In February,

2014, he was the subject of a *New York Times* article by David Gonzalez, "A Poet Mines Memories of Drug Addiction."

Lawrence Ferlinghetti was a poet, publisher and political iconoclast who, until his recent death at the age of 101, occupied a central position among the Beat generation writers. He inspired and nurtured generations of artists and American writers due not only to his enormously popular books *Coney Island of the Mind* (New Directions) and *Pictures of the Gone World* (City Lights), but his friendship and support for Ginsberg, Kerouac, Corso, Snyder, and countless other Beat and Post-Beat writers, from City Lights, his famed bookstore in North Beach, San Francisco. Like a number of other major 20th century poets in San Francisco, however, Ferlinghetti's origins were in NYC – he was born in Yonkers (his parents met in Coney Island) and raised in Bronxville.

Edward Field's career has been exclusively literary until recently – having published numerous books of poetry, fiction, memoirs, travel etc. But suddenly he has become a famous veteran – indeed, inducted into the Veterans Hall of Fame, since he was a gay soldier in World War II. A short film has been made of his being shot up over Berlin and his plane crashing into the North Sea. After the war he was witness to the modern history of Greenwich Village and its role as a birthplace of vivid literature and gay culture, and his memoir, *The Man Who Would Marry Susan Sontag and Other Intimate Literary Portraits of the Bohemian Era*, gives a glimpse into the lives of many personalities of the day. "Of course, as a New Yorker, being gay has always been as much a part of the city's make-up as the numerous ethnic populations, and why gay people flock here. And now it is a point of pride."

Karen Finneyfrock is the author of two young adult novels, *The Sweet Revenge of Celia Door* and *Starbird Murphy and the World Outside*, both published by Viking Children's Books. She is the author of the poetry collection, *Ceremony for the Choking Ghost*, and co-editor of the anthology *Courage: Daring Poems for Gutsy Girls* (Write Bloody Publishing). She's performed at several NYC spoken word venues including the reading series *Page Meets Stage*.

Stewart Florsheim grew up in Washington Heights, in upper Manhattan, the son of refugees from Hitler's Germany. He has been widely published in magazines and anthologies. Stewart was the editor of *Ghosts of the Holocaust*, an anthology of poetry by children of

Holocaust survivors (Wayne State University Press, 1989). He wrote the poetry chapbook, *The Girl Eating Oysters* (2River, 2004). In 2005, Stewart won the Blue Light Book Award for *The Short Fall From Grace* (Blue Light Press, 2006). His collection, *A Split Second of Light*, was published by Blue Light Press in 2011 and received an Honorable Mention in the San Francisco Book Festival, honoring the best books published in the Spring of 2011.

Kofi Fosu Forson is a theater director, art writer and artist who experiments with ambidexterity. He is published in *Maintenant 10*, Great Weather for Media's *Understanding Between Foxes and Light*, *Anti-Hero in Chic* (Full of Crow Press and Flapperhouse.) "I've lived in New York City since the late 70s and witnessed firsthand the latter stages of the punk movement, cafe scene of the 90s, and the relocation of the art galleries in the early 2000s from Soho to Chelsea.

Diane Frank is author of eight books of poems, three novels, and a photo memoir of her 400 mile trek in the Nepal Himalayas. She lives in San Francisco, where she dances, plays cello with the Golden Gate Symphony, and creates her life as an art form. Her new book, *While Listening to the Enigma Variations: New and Selected Poems*, was published in 2021 by Glass Lyre Press. "My grandmother lived on East 63rd Street, worked with Leonard Bernstein, and always made sure she had tickets for us to see children's concerts at the New York Philharmonic."

Philip Fried's mother, Mollie Green, grew up in an immigrant Jewish family on Manhattan's Lower East Side and spoke Yiddish before she spoke English. His father, Seymour Fried, lived in the Bronx and therefore, to the relatively poor Greens, had the aura of middle-class success. After serving in the army in Atlanta, Georgia, during the war, Seymour brought Mollie to the splendor of Parkchester, a new housing project for 50,000 people in the Bronx that was planned with four identical quadrants – each with a shuffleboard court, a playground, a circular park, buildings of 7 and 12 stories, and a police squadron whose main task was keeping kids off the grass. "This world seemed perfectly normal to me as I grew up, until I went to college in the Midwest and met people who thought it was strange." Today, he and his wife, the photographer Lynn Saville, live on Manhattan's Riverside Drive, a curving avenue more akin to the nearby Hudson River than to the borough's interior grid. He has published eight books of poetry, most recently *Squaring the Circle* (Salmon Poetry, Ireland, 2017), from which "The Quantum Mechanics of Everyday Life" comes, and *Among The Gliesians* (Salmon, 2020).

Thomas Fucaloro has helped in building a community of poets in Staten Island since 2010, focusing on making poetry accessible to all, either through the Life*Vest*Poetry Slam, The Who Needs Healing? Reading Series, or the free workshops offered at Staten Island Libraries and other various orgs.

Davidson Garrett has lived in New York City for almost half a century. A poet and actor, he drove a yellow taxi off and on for forty years to subsidize his artistic pursuits. He is the author of the poetry collection, *King Lear of the Taxi* (Advent Purple Press, 2006) and *Arias of a Rhapsodic Spirit* (Kelsay Books, 2020). He is a member of the PEN Worker Writers School.

Frank X. Gaspar is author of five poetry collections and three novels. His work has appeared widely in magazines and literary journals, including *The New Yorker*, *The Nation*, *The Harvard Review*, *The American Poetry Review*, and others. He currently teaches in the Graduate Writing Program at Pacific University, Oregon. "At seventeen, I left my home in Provincetown, Massachusetts, to move to New York City to become a writer. I lived for a time in Chelsea at 300 West 30th Street. It took a bit longer for me to become a writer than I thought it would."

Kat Georges is a New York City-based poet, playwright, and graphic designer. Author of *Our Lady of the Hunger: Poems* and *Three Somebodies: Plays about Notorious Dissidents*. She is co-founder of Three Rooms Press, and her greatest joy is to plug into the electricity of life and shoot hot sparks into the universe.

Phillip Giambri aka **"The Ancient Mariner"** left home at eighteen and never looked back. He's seen and done what others dream of or fear. His 2020 novelette *The Amorous Adventures of Blondie and Boho* is a story of love, survival, and gentrification in NYC's East Village where he's lived since 1971.

Robert Anthony Gibbons, a native Floridian, came to New York City in 2007 in search of his muse, Langston Hughes, and found a vibrant contemporary poetry community at the Cornelia Street Cafe, the Green Pavilion, Nomad's Choir, Brownstone Poets, Hydrogen JukeBox, Saturn Series, Parkside Lounge, and Phoenix among other venues. His first book, *Close to the Tree*, was published by the New York-based Three Rooms Press in 2012. He is an Obsidian Fellow (2019), a Cave Canem Fellow (2019-2021) and has received residencies from the Norman Mailer Foundation (2017) and the Disquiet International Literary Program (2018). In 2018 he completed his MFA at City College.

Tony Gloeggler is a life-long resident of New York City and managed group homes for the mentally challenged in Brooklyn for over 40 years. His first full length collection, *One Wish Left*, went into a 2nd printing in 2007. *Until the Last Light Leaves* was published with NYQ Books in 2015. Most recently, NYQ Books published *What Kind of Man* in 2020 and it was named as a finalist for the Paterson Poetry Prize 2021.

Philip Good helped publish the short lived mimeographed zine *Blue Smoke*. He lived for many years in lower Manhattan before relocating to upstate New York with Bernadette Mayer. They live near a small piece of woods they call the poetry state forest.

Meghan Grupposo has learned to do some things in her relatively short time as a human – garden, recommend a delicious wine, dance, choreograph, teach 30 some odd uninterested elementary school humans to also dance and even convince them that they like it. She's received many hugs, most of them in New York City. Her preferred form of processing existence is writing poetry. She's co-founder of the monthly NYC poetry reading, NeuroNautic Institute Presents, and her work can be found in the on-line 'zine *Polarity*, *Great Weather for Media's Escape Wheel*, and Three Rooms Press' Dada Journals, *Maintenant* 14 and 15.

George Guida is author of nine books, most recently *Posts from Suburbia: A Novel* (Encircle Publications, 2022), *Zen of Pop* (Long Sky Media, 2020), and the revised edition of *New York and Other Lovers* (Encircle Publications, 2020). A graduate of both Columbia College, Columbia University and the City University of New York Doctoral English Program, he lived in New York City for two decades, where he served as an officer of the Italian American Writers Association and curated the Bensonhurst Reading Series and the Lit Series at Smalls Jazz Club. He is currently teaching writing and literature at New York City College of Technology, curating the Finger Lakes Reading Series in Dansville, New York, and completing a novel set mainly in New York and a book about poetry communities across the U. S entitled *Virtue at the Coffee House*.

Janet Hamill is the author of nine books of poetry and short fiction: *A Map of the Heavens: Selected Poems 1975-2017, Real Fire, Knock, Tales from the Eternal Café, Body of Water, Lost Ceilings, Nostalgia of the Infinite, The Temple* and *Troublante.* Her poetry has been nominated for the Pushcart Prize and the William Carlos Williams Prize and *Tales from the Eternal Café* was named one of the "Best Books of 2014" by *Publishers Weekly.* She's taught at Naropa, Cabrillo College and New England College, where she received her MFA. At present, she is completing her first novel and awaiting publication of a new collection, *Baby Parade*, forthcoming from Vehicle Editions.

Nathalie Handal is a Queens-based poet. Her recent poetry books include *Life in A Country Album,* winner of the 2020 Palestine Book Award and finalist for the Foreword Book Award; the flash collection *The Republics,* winner of the Virginia Faulkner Award for Excellence in Writing, and the Arab American Book Award; the critically acclaimed *Poet in Andalucía;* and *Love and Strange Horses,* winner of the Gold Medal Independent Publisher Book Award. She is the author of eight plays, editor of two anthologies, and her flash essays and creative nonfiction have appeared in *Vanity Fair, Guernica Magazine, The Guardian, The New York Times, The Nation, The Irish Times,* among others. Handal is the recipient of awards from the PEN Foundation, the Lannan Foundation, Centro Andaluz de las Letras, Fondazione di Venezia, among others. She is a professor at New York University, and writes the literary travel column "The City and the Writer" for *Words without Borders* magazine.

Aimee Herman has been living in Brooklyn, NY for over ten years now. Live in New York long enough and you start to feel like a subway map, graffiti grazing bodies, the twists and turns of bodegas, museums and spontaneous poems howled into the air. An author of two books of poems and the novel, *Everything Grows,* Aimee is also a writing/ literature teacher at Bronx Community College, and co-founder of the poetry band Hydrogen Junkbox along with NYC poet David Lawton.

Diana Gitesha Hernández, aka *Gitesha* is an NYC poet, bred in Brooklyn, born in Santurce, Puerto Rico, and longtime resident of Loisada, Manhattan. Hernández, a multi-media performance artist, poet, jazz singer and drum percussionist, is the author of several collections of poetry: *Slingshot Luv* (1985); *Love Poems from a Nuyorican Princess Dreaming of Rimbaud* (1994); *Raw Lips Melao, a Nuyorican Rhapsody*

(2004); *Mango PI* (2008); *I Am a Muse* (2012) and *Hot Steam* (2018). Her poetry has been published in *Aloud!; Voices from the Nuyorican Poets Cafe* Anthology, and *Breaking Ground*, anthology of Puerto Rican Women Writers in New York 1980-2012. Her band's – Gitesha's Jazz Boogaloo (Latin), Orgasmic Orchestra (word distillery) and Soulful Distancing (jazz) performs regularly in NYC.

Robert Hershon, (1936-2021) who was born in Queens but lived most of his life in Brooklyn, was co-editor of Hanging Loose Press and *Hanging Loose* magazine. He is survived by his wife Donna Brook and daughter Elizabeth. Hershon published fourteen books of poetry. Most recently, *End of the Business Day* (2018), *Freeze Frame* (2015) *Goldfish and Rose* (2013); *Into a Punchline: Poems 1984-1994* (1994), *The German Lunatic* (2000), and *Calls from the Outside World* (2006). He wrote for the blogs of Best American Poetry and The Poetry Foundation and received two creative writing fellowships from the National Endowment for the Arts and three from the New York Foundation for the Arts. He served as the executive director of the Print Center for 35 years.

William Heyen is Professor of English and Poet in Residence Emeritus at SUNY Brockport. He was a Senior Fulbright Lecturer in American Literature in Germany, and has won NEA, Guggenheim, American Academy and Institute of Arts and Letters, Pushcart, and other awards. A National Book Award Finalist for his *Shoah Train* and the author of dozens of other books, his most recent are *Nature: Selected and New Poems 1970-2020* and *The Corona Clock* (both from Mammoth Books).

Scott Hightower is the author of four books of poetry in the US and two bilingual (English – Spanish) collections published in Madrid. He teaches at New York University at the Gallatin School, sojourns in Spain, and resides in Manhattan, where he enjoys wolfing down Reuben and Cuban sandwiches.

Ngoma Hill is a performance poet, multi-instrumentalist, singer/songwriter, artivist and paradigm shifter, who for over 50 years has used culture as a tool to raise socio-political and spiritual consciousness through work that encourages critical thought. A former member of Amiri Baraka's "The Spirit House Movers and Players" and the contemporary freedom song duo "Serious Bizness," Ngoma weaves poetry and song that raises contradictions and searches for a solution to a just and peaceful world. He can be seen dropping knowledge on New York City stages and beyond.

Edward Hirsch, a MacArthur Fellow, has published ten books of poems, most recently *Gabriel: A Poem* (2014) and *Stranger by Night* (2020), and six books about poetry, most newly, *100 Poems to Break Your Heart* (2021). He moved to New York in 2003 to become president of the John Simon Guggenheim Memorial Foundation and lives in Brooklyn.

Jack Hirschman (1933-2021) was born in The Bronx, December 13, 1933. He is an emeritus Poet Laureate of San Francisco, a founding member of the Revolutionary Poets Brigade of San Francisco, the Roque Dalton Cultural Brigade, The Jacques Roumain Cultural Brigade, and the World Poetry Movement. He has translated more women poets from other countries than any poet in the United States, among the more than 50 books of translations from 9 languages, including Neruda, Pasolini and Depestre. His own masterwork are 3 thousand-page, long-poem works called *The Arcanes*. He was immensely proud of having been with the Communist Labor Party from 1980-1992, and with the League of Revolutionaries for a New America that continues the struggle today.

Jane Hirshfield (1933-2021) was born in New York City. She learned to write, and to love writing from Mrs Barlow, her first grade teacher at P.S. 40 on East 20th St. At age eight, she bought her first book from the circular wire display rack of a stationery store on First Avenue, a Peter Pauper Press collection of Japanese haiku. Since then she has published nine poetry collections, most recently *Ledger* (NY: Knopf, 2020), two now classic books of essays, and four books collecting the work of the world's poets from the deep past. Her work appears in the *New Yorker, the Atlantic,* the *New York Times, The TLS, Poetry,* and has received the Poetry Center Book Award, the California Book Award, and fellowships from the Guggenheim and Rockefeller foundations and the NEA. A former chancellor of the Academy of American Poets, she was inducted in 2019 into the American Academy of Arts and Sciences.

Roxanne Hoffman runs the literary press Poets Wear Prada with Jack Cooper. Her words can be found in cyberspace, set to music, on the silver screen, and in print. Her elegiac poem "In Loving Memory," illustrated by Edward Odwitt, was released as a chapbook in 2011. Their second collaboration, *The Little Entomologist,* was published in 2018. Roxanne was born and raised in Manhattan, earned her B.A. and M.Phil. from NYU, worked on Wall Street for 20 years, at VNS-NY for another 14, and co-hosted "The Longest Running Bar Poetry Reading in the Village" with legendary Beat poet Brigid Murnaghan at The Back Fence.

Bob Holman, "Bowery Bob," lives above the Bowery Poetry Club that he founded in 2002 after stints with the Nuyorican Poets Café (Original Slam Master) and the St. Marks Poetry Project (founder, Poets Theater Festival). He's a native New Yorker from Harlan, KY. His work centers on the Oral Tradition; his interest in Hip Hop led him to Africa and collaborations with the griot Papa Susso including translations of jeliya poems in *Sing This One Back To Me* (Coffee House). His films on endangered languages and poetry aired on PBS: *Language Matters* (w/ David Grubin), *The United States of Poetry* (w/ Josh Blum and Mark Pellington). Founder, Mouth Almighty – Mercury Records, w/ Bill Adler and Sekou Sundiata.. Recent projects – books include *The Cutouts (Matisse)* (music: Keith Patchel, dance: Molissa Finley), *Life Poem, The Unspoken and India Journals* (for *Ginsberg's Karma*, a film by Ram Devineni). He was married for 25 years to Elizabeth Murray, 3 children, 5 grandchildren.

Marie Howe was born in 1950 in Rochester, New York. She worked as a newspaper reporter and teacher before receiving her MFA from Columbia University in 1983. She has served as a Chancellor of the Academy of American Poets and is poet in residence at the Cathedral of St John the Divine, NYC, NY.

Matthew Hupert is a writer, a multi-media artist, and that rare bird, a New York City native. He is a founder of the NeuroNautic Institute and of NeuroNautic Press, with 2 full length collections, *Ism Is a Retrovirus* and *Secular Pantheism*, as well as several chapbooks and anthology appearances. He hosts several poetry reading series, including the annual showcase for New York voices, Night in the Naked City, and the monthly series, NeuroNautic Institute Presents. He is a recipient of the 2020 New York Acker Award for Show Organizer and Host. "When I'm not writing I can be found cooking for my family."

Paolo Javier was born in the Philippines and grew up in Las Piñas, Metro Manila; Katonah, Westchester County; El-Ma'adi, Cairo; Burnaby and North Delta, Metro Vancouver. He is the former Queens Borough Poet Laureate (2010-2014). The recipient of a 2021 Rauschenberg Foundation Artist Grant, Paolo was a featured artist in Greater NY 2015 and Queens International 2018: Volumes. He is the author of five full-length books of poetry, including *O.B.B.*, a (weird postcolonial techno dream-pop) comics poem that also includes illustrations by Alex Tarampi and Ernest Concepcion, published by Nightboat Books (2021). He has produced three albums of sound poetry with Listening Center (David Mason), including the limited edition pamphlet – cassette *Ur'lyeh/Aklopolis* and the booklet – cassette, *Maybe the Sweet Honey Pours.*

Hettie Jones is alive and well in New York and happy to be so! She is author of three collections of poetry, and the first wife of Amiri Baraka, known as LeRoi Jones at the time of their marriage. While known for her poetry, she has received acclaim for her memoir, *How I Became Hettie Jones.* She started the literary magazine *Yugen* with her husband, ran a writing workshop at the New York State Correctional Facility for Women at Bedford Hills which published a nationally distributed collection, *Aliens at the Border.* Jones is a former chair of the PEN Prison Writing Committee.

Patricia Spears Jones "has steadily and quietly enriched the American poetic tradition with sophisticated and moving poems," said the citation from The Jackson Poetry Prize which she received in 2017. Author of *A Lucent Fire: New and Selected Poems* and three other full-length poetry collections, Jones migrations from Forrest City, Arkansas to New York City has brought about a bounty of poems, essays, editorial projects interviews and collaborations. Now living in Bed-Stuy, Brooklyn, she finds the city, this nation, the globe fascinating, terrifying and is grateful for all acts of grace and kindness. Her most recent publications are in *African American Poetry: 250 Years of Struggle and Song*, edited by Kevin Young; *The Brooklyn Rail, The New Yorker* and *Pangyrus.*

Pierre Joris fell in love with New York in 1967, and even though he has often been unfaithful to her, he has always returned to his favorite city, for keeps in 2008. Meanwhile he spent some 55 years moving between Europe, the US and North Africa, publishing over 80 books of poetry, essays, translations and anthologies – most recently *Fox-trails, -tales and -trots* (poems and proses, Black Fountain Press); the translations *Memory Rose into Threshold Speech: The Collected Earlier Poetry of Paul Celan* (FSG) and *Microliths: Posthumous Prose of Paul Celan* (Contra Mundum Press). In 2020 he published *A City Full of Voices: Essays on the Work of Robert Kelly* and a bit earlier: *Arabia (not so) Deserta* (Essays, Spuyten Duyvil Press, 2019), *Conversations in the Pyrenees* with Adonis (CMP 2018), and *The Book of U* (poems, with Nicole Peyrafitte, Editions Simoncini

2017). When not on the road, he lives in Bay Ridge, Brooklyn, with his wife, multimedia *praticienne* Nicole Peyrafitte; the two often collaborate on performance work they call *Domopoetic Actions.*

Jennifer Juneau is author of the novel, *ÜberChef USA* (Spork Press, 2019) and the poetry collection, *More Than Moon* (Is a Rose Press, 2020). Her work has been published in places such as *Cimarron Review, Columbia Journal, Passages North, Rattle, Seattle Review* and elsewhere. "After moving back to New York from Europe, my poetry had taken on a liberating, self-celebratory tone, that resonates with all the city's filth and beauty. Living among the magic of Manhattan's culture and nightlife has inspired me to seize the immediacy of the experience and put it into verse."

Ron Kolm is a contributing editor of *Sensitive Skin* magazine and is the author of *Divine Comedy, Duke & Jill, Suburban Ambush, Night Shift, A Change in the Weather, Welcome to the Barbecue* and *Swimming in the Shallow End.* He's had work in *And Then, Great Weather for Media, Maintenant, Live Mag!, Local Knowledge, NYSAI,* the *Poets of Queens* anthology, the *Riverside Poets Anthology* and the *Brownstone Poets* anthologies. Ron has worked in most of the important independent bookstores in New York City, including The Strand, Coliseum Books, St. Mark's Bookshop, Shakespeare and Company and Posman Books. His papers were purchased by the New York University Library. He's also involved with several other archives including the poetry archive at SUNY Buffalo and the main Ohio State University Library.

Yusef Komunyakaa's books of poetry include *Taboo, Dien Cai Dau, Neon Vernacular,* for which he received the Pulitzer Prize, *Thieves of Paradise, Pleasure Dome, Talking Dirty to the Gods, Warhorses, The Chameleon Couch, Testimony, The Emperor of Water Clocks,* and most recently, *Everyday Mojo Songs of Earth.* His honors include the William Faulkner Prize (Université Rennes, France), the Ruth Lilly Poetry Prize, and the 2011 Wallace Stevens Award. His plays, performance art and libretti have been performed internationally and include *Saturnalia, Testimony, Gilgamesh,* and *Wakonka's Dream.* Komunyakaa served as New York State Poet 2016-2018; and he retired 2021 as Senior Poet and Global Professor at New York University.

Ptr Kozlowski drove a cab out of the legendary Dover Garage on Hudson Street in the 1980s – from Studio 54 to the Mineshaft, all viewed from curbside. With that and other driving jobs, and some time setting type in a letterpress shop, he supported a music and poetry habit. He played guitar, sang and wrote songs with JD Rage in a New Wave band called Baby Boom that played at A7, CBGB's and the SIN Club, and put out an EP, "Basket Case," in 1984. Now living in Brooklyn, he has read at Bowery Poetry Club, ABC No Rio, Yippie Museum Cafe, Cornelia St. Cafe, Boog City Festival, Barnes and Noble Park Slope, the Conklin Barn in Huntington, L.I. and other NYC area venues.

Michael Lally "Born in New Jersey in 1942, the youngest of seven in an Irish-American family and clan of cops, priests, politicians, teachers, poets, and musicians, my earliest memory of Manhattan is of my mother taking pre-school me to a matinee movie and stage show at the Paramount Theater while my siblings were in school. From that moment til now, New York has always been my heart's home (and more specifically at times in the 1950s and '60s it was The Village, East and West, and The Lower Eastside and Brooklyn, and in the 1970s, '80s, and '90s add what would become Soho and Tribeca, and at times in this century add the Upper Westside)." His 30th and latest book, *Another Way To Play: Poems 1960-2017* (7 Stories Press), contains poems about NYC in all those periods and neighborhoods.

Inmaculada Lara-Bonilla is a poet, fiction, and essay writer. Her poetry, written in English and Spanish, has been published in journals such as *Stone Canoe, Literal Magazine, ViceVersa, Enclave, Híbrido literario, Mantis, Nueva York Poetry Review,* and is included in the anthologies *Luna y panorama en los rascacielos* (2019, 2021), *Poetry Fighters* (2022) and *Viento del norte. Antología de poetas hispanos en Nueva York* (2022). Her short stories and chronicles have appeared in *Zenda Libros* and *ViceVersa*. She teaches Latinx Literature at Hostos CC (CUNY) in the Bronx, where she is also the Institute of Latin American Writers's Director and Editor of its literary journal, *Hostos Review/Revista Hostosiana*. She lives by the Hudson River, the city's ultimate navigable frontier.

Pamela L. Laskin is a native-grown New Yorker (Queens, NYC), who has continued to love New York through the decades – even at its worst. She is director of The Poetry Outreach Center of the City University of New York, where she teaches Children's Writing to graduate and undergraduate students. She is a published author of five books of poetry and three young adult novels. *The Secret Language of Crazy*, a middle grade novel, will be published in Fall, 2021. *Ronit and Jamil*, a Palestinian/Israeli Romeo and Juliet (published by Harper Collins in 2017) is currently being adapted for the stage.

David Lawton moved to New York City from his native Boston in the summer of 1984. While part of the scene at the Chelsea Hotel he befriended Beat godfather Herbert Huncke and San Francisco poet Marty Matz, deepening his interest in the Beat tradition. Besides his own writing, David has been involved as a host and curator of poetry events in NYC since he co-produced *Downtown Does Huncke* for His Birthday with his friend Dimitri Mugianis in January 2009.

Jane LeCroy grew up in Nyack, New York, outside NYC. A pink bubble on the skyline was visible every night as the view from her childhood bed. It was her intention to live in that pink bubble when she grew up, it was the light of NYC. She moved there to attend Eugene Lang college in 1991, and has lived there ever since, writing poetry and music, performing her work, and teaching poetry to youth through the amazing non-profit, Uptown Stories, in Washington Heights. You can hear her records on your favorite streaming platform, her different lyrically-driven bands on Imaginator Records are: The Icebergs (cello and drums), Ohmslice (spontaneous music with modular synth and pencilina), and her newest project, the rock band, Shelter Puppy. Her book of lyric poems, *Signature Play* is on Three Rooms Press. The Library of Congress has her DNA, as her first chapbook, *Names*, from the Art House Booklyn, was bound with her hair and is in their collection.

David Lehman was born in New York City and educated at Stuyvesant High School and Columbia University. His recent books include *One Hundred Autobiographies: A Memoir* (Cornell University Press, 2019) and *Playlist: A Poem* (University of Pittsburgh Press, 2019). A new book of poems, *The Morning Line*, was scheduled to be published by the University of Pittsburgh Press in Fall 2021.

Jean Lehrman writes about pain, rage and courage in modern New York City life. A popular poet and performer in New York City, she is published in several local journals, including *Clown Wars* and anthologized in *Cat's Breath* (Rogue Scholars Press, 2005). Her chapbooks include: *If You Come Back I Won't Have AIDS* (Dead Proofreaders Society, 2004) and *Lazarus* (Rogue Scholar Press 2007).

Linda Lerner states: "I'm a New York City writer in the sense that my poems, no matter the subject, are rooted in this city I was born in, and whose rhythm my poems pick up. Here there is always something to worry about. Covid is going away; crime is coming back. The excitement and energy are coming back too, and I'm back riding the F train again on and off the page, masked or unmasked, an escape artist, a survivor." NYQ Books published three of her collections, most recent, *Taking the F train*, 2021.

M. L. Liebler first came to New York City in 1971 as a teenager. He spent two weeks in the Village visiting The Fillmore, and he discovering Gil Scott Heron's poetry on vinyl at Bleeker Bob's. He finally returned as a published poet in 1990 to read everywhere from St. Mark's to the Knitting Factory on Houston, The Nuyorican Café, The Right Bank in Brooklyn, The YMCA's West Side Writer's Voice and City College. Liebler is an internationally known and widely published Detroit poet, university professor, literary arts activist and arts organizer. He is the author of 15 books and chapbooks and has been St. Clair Shores (his hometown) first Poet Laureate since 2005. His newest anthology, *Respect: Poets on Detroit Music* edited by M. L. Liebler and Jim Daniels (Michigan State University Press 2020), just received the 2021 Library of Michigan Notable Book Award. Forthcoming is an album of poetry and music entitled *The Moon a Box for Record Store Day* (2021 by M. L. Liebler and Al Kooper.) "I first saw Faruq Z. Bey do poetry and music at The Orange Bear and The Bowery Poetry Club in early 2002."

Maria Lisella is the sixth Queens Poet Laureate and the author of the collection, *Thieves in the Family*, and two chapbooks, *Amore on Hope Street* and *Two Naked Feet*. Named a 2020 Poets Laureate Fellow by the Academy of American Poets, she co-curates the Italian American Writers Association (IAWA) series, now in its 30th year in New York; the second series is Boston-based and curated by Julia Lisella and Jennifer Martelli. As a journalist, she is the NY Culture editor for the *Jerusalem Post* and contributes to the online bilingual publication, *La Voce di New York*.

Ellaraine Lockie is a nonfiction book and flash fiction author, essayist and poet with fourteen published chapbooks. Her connection to NYC reaches back to childhood in a small wheat-farming town in Montana. "I was eight when the state's newspaper headlined on its front page, "NYC Cab Driver Kills Woman Pedestrian on Sidewalk." People talked about

312

it for weeks, warning others never to go to NYC. I decided ten years ago I that I wouldn't overcome such a long-existing, irrational fear by going there as a tourist, and that I had to actually live there for a time. So in 2011 I rented an apartment in Soho for a month, fell in love, and have lived in various apartments in different areas for a month nearly every year since." She's currently writing a poetry collection inspired by what has become her favorite city.

Maya Mahmud is a poet and mixed-media artist living in Crown Heights, Brooklyn. There she spends her days writing, painting, and listening to the music booming from the street below her bedroom window. She studied Mass Media and Communication at NYU. She is the Communications Manager for Audivita Studios, an audiobook and podcast production company. Her poetry and studio art has appeared in *Brio, Literary Journal, Frontier Poetry,* and *2 Horatio.*

Paul Mariani was born in Astoria and lived in Manhattan until he was eight, when his family made its way out to the broad open plains of Levittown's potato farms and then Mineola. Schooled at Chaminade HS, Manhattan College, Colgate and CCNY, where he earned his PhD in English Lit and Comparative Literature before being sent to "the provinces" of Massachusetts – (U Mass-Amherst and Boston College (poetry chair) until retirement at age 76), he taught at Hunter, Lehman College, and the John Jay College of Criminal Justice at the Police Academy, where he met Frank Serpico. An experimental film based on his bio of Hart Crane, entitled "The Broken Tower," was made by James Franco. "And here's the thing: often in the evening, I'm a six-year-old kid again, walking down to the park at Turtle Bay, where I stare out at the river as the evening sky grows darker and darker and the gulls still cry out, asking questions I cannot answer."

Julio Marzán was born in San Juan and, at the age of four months, was brought to New York City, where he completed all his studies (Fordham, B.A., Columbia, M.F.A, and New York University, Ph.D.). He served on the Governing Board of Poets House as well on its original Advisory Panel. He has published two poetry books, *Translations without Originals* (I. Reed Books (1986) and, in Spanish, *Puerta de Tierra* (Editorial U. P.R., 1998), and forthcoming is *The Glue Trap and Other Poems* (Fernwood Press). Selections in the college texts, *The Bedford Introduction to Literature, The Bedford Introduction to Poetry, Latino Boom,* among others. His poems have been published in *New Letters, Parnassus, Ploughshares, Tin House, 3 Quarks Daily,* and *Harper's Magazine,* among others. 2004-2007 Poet Laureate of Queens, Martín Espada requested permission to reprint the title and epigraph poem, "Don't Let Me Die in Disneyland" (the title of his second novel), in the anthology, *What Saves Us. Poems of Empathy and Outrage in the Age of Trump.*

Mindy Matijasevic, a lifetime New Yorker, specifically a Bronx gal, writes poetry, memoir, and her comedy material. She is a two-time recipient of a B.R.I.O. (Bronx Recognizes Its Own) Award from the Bronx Council on the Arts – once for nonfiction literature, and once for poetry. Her work has appeared in many print and on-line journals, most recently *Home Planet News* Online Issue 8.

Bernadette Mayer, born 1945 in Brooklyn, NY, is the author of over thirty books including the acclaimed *Midwinter Day* (1982), a book-length poem written during a single day in Lenox, Massachusetts. From 1980-1984, she served as the director of the St. Mark's Poetry Project. To learn more visit bernadettemayer.com.

Jesús Papoleto Meléndez, born and raised, run-away, exiled, then returned, Nuyorican-Native-New Yorker, is an award-winning poet who is recognized as one of the founders of the Nuyorican Movement. He is also a playwright, teacher, activist and presently, actor. Meléndez began publishing his first poems in the late 1960's and has continued with *Hey Yo! Yo Soy! 40 Years of Nuyorican Street Poetry* (2012); *Papolítico, Poems of a Political Persuasion* (2018); and most recently, *Borracho* (Very Drunk) – *Love Poems and Other Acts of Madness* (2020, 2LeafPress). His work has been anthologized in numerous publications, recently in *Pa'lante a La Luz – Charge into the Light* (Rogue Scholars Press, 2018), *Word, An Anthology by A Gathering of the Tribes* (2017), and *Manteca, An Anthology of Afro-Latin@ Poets* (Arte Publico Press, 2017). Meléndez is a NYFA Poetry Fellow (New York Foundation for the Arts, 2001), and now an elder statesman of the New York poetry scene.

Nancy Mercado most recently edited a special section celebrating the life of the late founder of the Nuyorican Poets Cafe, Miguel Algarín, appearing in *KONCH Magazine* this Spring 2022. She is the recipient of the 2017 American Book Award for Lifetime Achievement presented by the Before Columbus Foundation. Mercado was named one of 200 living individuals who best embody the work and spirit of Frederick

Douglass (on the bicentennial of his birth) by the Frederick Douglass Family Initiatives and the Antiracist Research and Policy Center at American University. Her critique of West Side Story appears in Bigotry on Broadway (Baraka Books). "From childhood, I was fascinated by New York City and dreamt of living here. I achieved that dream."

Sharon Mesmer moved to Brooklyn, NY from Chicago, IL in 1988 and in spite of all odds – plagues, failed banks, fascist presidents, irate neighbors – is still living here. Her most recent poetry collection, *Greetings From My Girlie Leisure Place* (Bloof Books) was voted Best of 2015 by *Entropy* magazine. Her fiction collections include *Ma Vie à Yonago* from Hachette, in French translation. Her essays, reviews and interviews have appeared in the *The New York Times, New York Magazine/The Cut, Paris Review, American Poetry Review, Wall Street Journal* and *The Brooklyn Rail*, among others. She teaches creative writing at NYU and the New School.

David Mills holds an MFA from Warren Wilson College. He's published three collections, *The Dream Detective, The Sudden Country, Boneyarn* and *After Mistic*. His poems have appeared in *Ploughshares, Brooklyn Rail, Colorado Review, The Common, Crab Orchard Review, Jubilat, Callaloo, Obsidian, Brooklyn Rail, Aloud: Live from the Nuyorican Poets Cafe and Fence*. He has also received fellowships from the New York Foundation for the Arts, Pan African Literary Forum, Breadloaf, The American Antiquarian Society and the Lannan Foundation. He lived in Langston Hughes' landmark Harlem home.

Gloria Mindock visits NYC regularly to read at venues, see performance art, theatre, and to see friends. She is the author of *Ash* (Glass Lyre Press), *I Wish Francisco Franco Would Love Me* (Nixes Mate Books), *Whiteness of Bone* (Glass Lyre Press), *La Portile Raiului*, translated into Romanian by Flavia Cosma (Ars Longa Press, Romania), *Nothing Divine Here* (U Šoku Štampa, Montenegro), and *Blood Soaked Dresses* (Ibbetson St. Press). Widely published in the USA and abroad, Gloria is editor of Červená Barva Press and was the Poet Laureate in Somerville, MA in 2017 and 2018. "The best thing is that NYC never closes, and places are open all night."

Thurston Moore born 1958, moved to NYC 1976, started Sonic Youth 1980, edited the fanzines *Killer, Sonic Death,* and *Ecstatic Peace Poetry Journal*, started Ecstatic Peace records and tapes label, senior editor of

Ecstatic Peace Library, and *Flowers and Cream*, edited books at Rizzoli and Abrams, on faculty at the Naropa University summer writing program since 2011, published through various imprints, worked collaboratively with Yoko Ono, Merce Cunningham, Cecil Taylor, Rhys Chatham, Lydia Lunch, John Zorn, Takehisa Kosugi and Glenn Branca, composed music for films by Olivier Assayas, Gus Van Sant, and Allison Anders, records and tours both solo, with various ensembles and with his own band, resides everywhere.

Frank Murphy was born and grew up in the South Bronx. He began writing poetry while stationed in Korea and joined the New York poetry scene in the early sixties. He is the author of five books of poetry and has been published in three New York anthologies as well as many magazines. His book, *A Christmas Poem*, illustrated by the Dutch artist, Corina Teunissen van Manen, was recently republished as *A Fisherman's Dream*. He co-edited the New York City Poetry Calendar for sixteen years and is now chief-editor of *Home Planet News*.

Eileen Myles came to New York City in 1974 from Boston to be a poet. They've lived in the East Village since 1977, as well as living in Marfa TX since 2015 and have published 22 books – most recently *For Now*, a talk/essay about writing (and New York real estate) from Yale Press.

Claudine Nash is a Bronx-based psychologist and an award-winning poet who has authored five poetry collections. She was chosen winner of the 2020 Blue Light Book Award for her poetry collection *Beginner's Guide to Loss in the Multiverse*. "I grew up in the ethnically and linguistically diverse borough of Queens where 138 languages are spoken. However, like many, I am still guilty of referring to Manhattan as "The City" and used to take the 7 train to get there."

Uche Nduka is an Okijan by birth and a New Yorker by choice. In this scenario of community and self-creation, he has written 12 volumes of poetry of which the latest are *Living in Public* (2018) and *Facing You* (2020). His writing has been translated into German, Italian, Finnish, Arabic etc. He presently teaches and argues at CUNY.

Urayoán Noel is from Río Piedras, Puerto Rico, and lives in the South Bronx, under the shadow of the Bruckner Expressway and a few blocks from where his maternal great-grandmother lived (now a community garden) upon migrating from Puerto Rico in the pre-expressway days. A professor at NYU, he is the author of several poetry collections, most recently *Transversal* (2021) and *Buzzing Hemisphere / Rumor Hemisférico* (2015), both from the University of Arizona Press, and of the critical study, *In Visible Movement: Nuyorican Poetry from the Sixties to Slam* (University of Iowa Press, 2014), winner of the LASA Latino Studies Book Prize. As a translator of Latin American poetry, he has been a finalist for the National Translation Award and the Best Translated Book Award.

Charles North was born in Brooklyn and has lived and taught in NYC most of his life. His publications include a dozen books of poems, books of essays, and collaborations with artists. *What It Is Like* (2011) headed NPR's Best Poetry Books of the Year, and *Everything and Other Poems* (2020) was named a NY Times New and Noteworthy Book. North has received a Fund for Contemporary Arts Award, two NEA grants, four Fund for Poetry awards, and a Poets Foundation Award. "With New York poet James Schuyler, I edited the anthologies *Broadway* and *Broadway 2*, mixing New York (mostly) poets and painters. At the time the idea was hatched, both of us were living on Broadway."

D. Nurkse has taught poetry at Rikers Island, Sarah Lawrence College MFA, and dozens of venues in between. He is a former Brooklyn Poet Laureate.

Kimberly Nunes received her MFA from Sarah Lawrence College in 2013. She lives in Marin County and Carmel by the Sea CA and has spent some years of her life in NYC, in her early career, and later as a graduate student and writer. "I know some wonderful poets there as well as I sit on the board of Four Way Books. I like to visit New York often, for meetings, to look at art, to see friends, to become inspired, whenever I can."

Obsidian is a poet from the Bronx, who began his career as a part of the Manhattan poetry scene during the early 90's. He's hosted, co-hosted, read, performed, taught poetry classes at CUNY, published and has been featured on radio, including NPR "This American Life." Right now he's mob deep in finishing a novel entitled, *Bottom Feeder and The Rise of The Mealy Men*. So don't stray too far...

Valery Oisteanu is a poet, writer and artist. Born in the USSR (1943) and educated in Romania, he adopted Dada and Surrealism as a philosophy or life and art in the early 1960s and immigrated to New

York City in 1972. He has authored 18 books of poetry as well as a forthcoming collection of essays titled *The Avant-Gods*. The recipient of the Kathy Acker Award (2013) for contribution to the American avant-garde in poetry performance, he takes part in theatrical and other poetry-musical collaborations with jazz artist from around the world in seasons he dubs "Jazzoetry."

Jane Ormerod is a poet, artist, and publisher. Born on the south coast of England, she has made New York City home since 2002. After arriving in New York, Jane made it her mission to attend a spoken word open mic every night and so discovered a community of intense talent, passion, support, and friendship. She is the author of the full-length poetry collections *Welcome to the Museum of Cattle* and *Recreational Vehicles on Fire* (both from Three Rooms Press), is a recipient of a 2020 Acker Award for publishing, and is a founding editor at great weather for MEDIA.

Alicia Ostriker is a poet and critic born and raised in New York who has written many poems about the city celebrating its vitality and diversity. She served as New York State Poet Laureate 2018-2021.

Yuko Otomo, a visual artist and a bilingual writer of Japanese origin, writes poetry, haiku, art criticism and essays. Her publications include *Garden: Selected Haiku* (Beehive Press); *Small Poems* (Ugly Duckling Presse); *STUDY and Other Poems on Art* (UDP); *KOAN* (New Feral Press); *FROZEN HEATWAVE: a collaborative linked poem project with Steve Dalachinsky* (Luna Bisonte Prods); and the most recent *Anonymous Landscape* (Lithic Press). She moved to NYC in 1979 and still lives in the downtown tenement apartment where she lived with her late husband poet, Steve Dalachinsky, for over 40 years.

Abiodun Oyewole was born Charles Davis in Cincinnati and grew up in Queens. He is a founding member of the American music and spoken-word group The Last Poets. Listening to his parents' jazz and gospel records and studying Langston Hughes and other great poets in school helped nurture his love of poetry. His mother taught him to "throw his voice" by making him recite the Lord's Prayer in their basement so that she could hear him in the kitchen. He took the name Oyewole at the age of fifteen years, after he and a friend went into a Yoruban Temple in Harlem. During the course of his fifty year career and his long affiliation with The Last Poets, Oyewole is one of several poets credited for liberating American poetry by creating open, vocal, spontaneous, energetic and uncensored vernacular verse that paved the way for spoken word and hip-hop.

Ron Padgett's *How Long* was a Pulitzer Prize finalist in poetry and his *Collected Poems* won the *LA Times* Prize for the best poetry book of 2014 and the William Carlos Williams Award from the Poetry Society of America. His translations include *Zone: Selected Poems of Guillaume Apollinaire* and Blaise Cendrars' *Complete Poems*. Seven of his poems were used in Jim Jarmusch's film, *Paterson*. Padgett's most recent collection is *Big Cabin* (Coffee House Press). New York City has been his home base since 1960.

Gregory Pardlo is the author of *Totem*, winner of the American Poetry Review / Honickman Prize, and *Digest*, winner of the Pulitzer Prize for Poetry. He is the recipient of fellowships from the New York Public Library's Cullman Center, the Guggenheim Foundation, the New York Foundation for the Arts, and a fellowship for translation from the National Endowment for the Arts. He is Poetry Editor for *Virginia Quarterly Review* and teaches in the MFA program at Rutgers University-Camden. His most recent book is *Air Traffic*, a memoir in essays. He lives in Bedford Stuyvesant, Brooklyn with his wife and two daughters.

Heeyen Park is a New School poet raised in Avenue U and Kings Highway, crossing the Brooklyn Bridge in energetic adventure headed to Elmer Homes Bobst Library in Union Square. She currently enjoys tanning by the pool in San Jose, where despite the humidity she waits for her Q train to 32nd Street in a floral maxi dress as she dabs sweat with her handkerchief made from South Korea.

Charles Pellegrino is a long time member of Local 638 Steamfitters. His poetry is formed and shaped by Trade Unionist history and the lure of the natural world. He's recently published in *No Distance Between Us – an Anthology of Italian American Poets*.

Simon Perchik is an attorney whose poems have appeared in *Partisan Review, Forge, Poetry, Osiris, The New Yorker* and elsewhere. "As a resident of NYC for over 25 years and a constant visitor to date, I consider myself a New Yorker to the bone. Especially because of my frequent visits to the NYPL for books I need for my writing that can be found nowhere else."

Puma Perl is the author of two chapbooks, *Ruby True* and *Belinda and Her Friends*, and three full-length poetry collections: *Knuckle Tattoos*, *Retrograde* (great weather for MEDIA), and *Birthdays Before and After* (Beyond Baroque Books.) She is the creator, curator, and host of Puma's Pandemonium, which brings spoken word together with rock and roll. Recipient of the 2016 Acker Award in the category of writing, her life is a Lower East Side film with a score provided by The Velvet Underground. "I spent my early years plotting my escape from Gravesend, Brooklyn, and have lived in Lower Manhattan most of my life, except for the random decade that I screwed up."

Simon Pettet is a long-time resident of New York's Lower East Side having arrived there in 1977 from London, England. John Ashbery amusingly referred to him as "a former English waif, but for decades a pillar of the St Mark's Poetry Project, the core of all that is New York about the New York School." More about him and his poems can be found on line at simonpettet.com.

Nicole Peyrafitte is a pluridisciplinary artist born in the French Pyrénées who now lives in Bay Ridge, Brooklyn. "No matter the season or the weather, I venture to the outskirts of the city, hiking, birding, swimming with my husband and collaborator Pierre Joris."

Wanda Phipps is a writer and translator originally from Washington, DC but who has lived in twenty or so different neighborhoods in the NYC area over a period of forty years. Her books include *Field of Wanting: Poems of Desire*, *Wake-Up Calls: 66 Morning Poems*, and *Mind Honey*. Her poetry has been translated into Ukrainian, Hungarian, Arabic, Galician and Bangla. She has received awards from the New York Foundation for the Arts, the National Theater Translation Fund, and others. As a founding member of Yara Arts Group she has collaborated on numerous theatrical productions presented in Ukraine, Kyrgyzstan, Siberia, and at La MaMa, E.T.C. in NYC. She's curated reading series at the Poetry Project at St. Mark's Church and written about the arts for *Boog City*, *Time Out New York*, *Paper Magazine*, and others.

Meg Pokrass is the author of seven flash fiction collections and recipient of the Blue Light Book Award twice, for *Cellulose Pajamas* (Blue Light Press, 2015) and *Spinning to Mars* (Blue Light Press, 2020). Her work has appeared in hundreds of literary journals and anthologies and has been published in two Norton anthologies of the flash fiction form: *Flash*

Fiction International (W.W. Norton, 2015) and *New Micro* (W.W. Norton, 2018). She is the Founder of *New Flash Fiction Review* and Founding Co-Editor of *Best Microfiction*. In 1987-1990, Meg lived in Hell's Kitchen and other parts of the city, auditioning for plays and working at many strange part-time jobs.

Michael Puzzo is a playwright, actor, director and member of NYC's legendary LAByrinth Theater Company since 1997. Some of his plays include; *Spirits of Exit Eleven*, *Lyric is Waiting*, *5 Sandwiches* and the NY Fringe Festival breakout hit, *The Dirty Talk*, which has been produced all over the world. "A 25 year East Village resident, I usually can be found hanging out with my wife Michelle and our dog Bobito at the Tile Bar on the corner of East 7th & 1st Avenue. We usually sit near the back."

Bob Quatrone has been host of NYC's 4 Horse poets' reading series and published such collections as *14 Poems in the Aquarian* (1980) and *The Fall of the Second Tower in the Unbearables* (2017.) He is Woodrow Wilson Fellow, Columbia U, 1967. "George Stade was chairman of the English Department at Columbia College and my doctoral advisor. He greatly liked my masters essay on Yeats and my early poetry, and made me his alter ego (Chi Chi Quatrone) in his outrageous novel *The Confessions of a Lady Killer*, which he was writing while he was my advisor."

Stuart P. Radowitz grew up in Brooklyn in the 1960s. His first collection, a ten-year compilation, is entitled *Snow Hangs on the Branches of Evergreens* and was recently published by Blue Light Press. "Growing up, Friday nights were often spent walking down Kings Highway, looking at girls and in store windows at clothing I couldn't afford, or sitting in Jahn's Ice Cream Parlor around the corner from Nostrand Avenue and Erasmus High School."

Charles Rammelkamp is Prose Editor for BrickHouse Books in Baltimore. A poetry chapbook, *Mortal Coil*, was published in January by Clare Songbirds Publishing. "Though I've lived in Baltimore for almost four decades, I've always felt New York was part of the larger neighborhood, just up the street – friends, family, poetry events, even work assignments, from SoHo and Greenwich Village to the West 70's and Columbia. Indeed, when the planes struck the towers, we pretty much immediately called family to see if everyone was alright."

Juana M. Ramos was born in Santa Ana, El Salvador, and currently lives in New York City where she is a professor of Spanish and literature at

York College, the City University of New York. "The subway is where I most intensely experience NYC. In fact, I do my best thinking on the J train!" She has participated in international poetry festivals and recitals in Mexico, Colombia, the Dominican Republic, Honduras, Cuba, Puerto Rico, El Salvador, Argentina, Guatemala, and Spain; and has published several books of poetry, including most recently, *Sin ambages/To the Point* (Cuadernos Negros Editorial, 2020). She is coauthor of *Tomamos la palabra: mujeres en la guerra civil de El Salvador (1980-1992)*, a collection of testimonies of women who fought in El Salvador's civil war.

Nicca Ray is the author of two books, the memoir, *Ray by Ray: A Daughter's Take on the Legend of Nicholas Ray* (Three Rooms Press) and the poetry collection, *Back Seat Baby* (Poison Fang Books). Her poetry has recently appeared in *Maintenant 15* (Three Rooms Press), *Paper Teller Diorama* (Great Weather for Media) and in *Love Love #4*. She is a 2020 Acker Award recipient for memoir and a Pushcart Prize nominee.

Eugene Richie is the author of the poetry collections *Moiré*; *Island Light*; *Only Here, Between*; and with Rosanne Wasserman, *Place du Carousel* and *Psyche and Amor*. He has edited John Ashbery's *Selected Prose*; three collections of Ashbery's translations of Pierre Martory's poems, with Wasserman and Olivier Brossard; and Ashbery's two-volume *Collected French Translations*, with Wasserman. He is a founding editor of The Groundwater Press and Pace University New York English Department Director of Creative Writing. 'After Red Noir' was written for Anne Waldman, after I participated in an interactive-audience performance of her play-poem *Red Noir*, in a little theater on the Lower East Side in New York City."

Thaddeus Rutkowski has lived in New York City, mainly in Manhattan, for more than forty years. He is the author of seven books, most recently *Tricks of Light*, a poetry collection. He teaches at Medgar Evers College and received a fiction writing fellowship from the New York Foundation for the Arts.

Eero Ruuttila has never really been a New Yorker unless sleeping on floors, couches, or the occasional well-made bed in The Lower East Side or Brooklyn counts. Read poetry at The Bowery Poetry Club, The Gershwin Hotel, A Gathering of Tribes Gallery, Oasis Lounge. Guest edited *The Café Review's* 2019 Winter issue. 35 years as an organic farmer and educator at Northeast Farms and/or Research Facilities. He likes to wear a camera.

Jerome Sala moved to New York from Chicago for the weather. He and his spouse, poet Elaine Equi, got to the city in '88, missing most of the happenings people speak about with great enthusiasm. This may be for the best, as it is said a sense of belatedness is crucial to all poets. He is the author of eight collections of poems, including cult classics such as *I Am Not a Juvenile Delinquent*, *Look Slimmer Instantly*, *The Cheapskates* and others. His most recent book is *Corporations Are People, Too!*; forthcoming is *How Much? New and Selected Poems* (both from NYQ Books). His blog on poetry and pop culture is *espresso bongo* https://espressobongo.typepad.com.

Nicole Santalucia is the author of *The Book of Dirt* (NYQ Books, 2020), *Spoiled Meat* (Headmistress Press, 2019), and *Because I Did Not Die* (Bordighera Press, 2015). She is a recipient of the Charlotte Mew Chapbook Prize and the Edna St. Vincent Millay Poetry Prize. Her work has appeared in publications such as *The Best American Poetry*, *The Rumpus*, *Columbia Journal*, as well as other places. She is an Associate Professor at Shippensburg University and has led poetry workshops in prisons, public libraries, Boys and Girls Clubs, and nursing homes. Santalucia loves going for long walks in Riverside Park and feeding the pigeons of the Upper West Side.

Annie Petrie Sauter was named Beat Poet Laureate from NY/ Colorado by the Beat Poetry Festival for 2017-19. "I lived in NYC starting at 9. I was in there all the time, I hit Zappa with my purse when I was 15. Then the Fugs and I worked on the Rat and EVO and blah blah blah. Spent time in women's house of D and the tombs. I got the grand tour."

Ilka Scobie is a native New Yorker who, post pandemic, is thrilled to be back teaching poetry in the public school system. Spuyten Duyvil has just published her book *Any Island*. She writes for *London Artlyst*, *American Book Review* and is an editor of *Live Mag!*. Desiderius Erasmus was a formative and early influence.

Robert Scotellaro was born and raised in East Harlem, NY. He has also lived in Queens, the Bronx, and Manhattan's Lower East Side. He currently lives in San Francisco where he can still be seen wearing a *Yankees* hat (one of many). Robert's work has been included in W.W. Norton's *Flash Fiction International*, *Gargoyle*, *Matter Press*, *New World*

Writing, Best Small Fictions 2016, 2017, and 2021, *Best Microfiction 2020*, and elsewhere. He is the author of seven literary chapbooks, several books for children, and five flash and micro story collections. He has, along with James Thomas, co-edited *New Micro: Exceptionally Short Fiction*, published by W.W. Norton & Co. Robert is one of the founding donors to *The Ransom Flash Fiction Collection* at the University of Texas, Austin.

Christopher Seid was born and raised in Iowa. After receiving his MFA from Vermont College in 1986, he moved to Brooklyn where he worked in advertising for seven years—before moving with his family to Portland, Maine. He has published two books of poetry, *Prayers to the Other Life*, which won the Marianne Moore Poetry Prize in 1997, published by Helicon Nine Editions, and *Age of Exploration*, which was selected for the Blue Light Press award in 2015. He currently lives in the Hudson Valley and works as a writer and editor.

Alan Semerdjian, Armenian-American poet, musician, and educator, was born in Woodside, Queens, and most recently lived in Manhattan's East Village for a decade with his partner, who is from Gravesend, Brooklyn, and their son. He misses the birds of Avenue A the most.

Vijay Seshadri is the author of five books of poems, most recently, *That Was Now, This Is Then* (Graywolf Press), and many essays, memoir fragments, and reviews. Born in India in 1954, he moved to North America at the end of that decade, and has lived in New York City for forty years, and in Brooklyn for thirty-five of those years. He teaches at Sarah Lawrence College.

Julie Sheehan's three poetry collections are *Bar Book*, *Orient Point* and *Thaw*. Her poems have appeared in many magazines and anthologies, including *Kenyon Review*, *The New Republic*, *The New Yorker*, *Parnassus*, *Prairie Schooner*, and *The Best American Poetry*. She teaches creative writing at Stony Brook and during 12 years in New York, lived in eight different apartments, only one of which was repeatedly burglarized.

Danny Shot was born in the Bronx and "spent my twenties in the East Village down the block from Allen Ginsberg, back when it was cool." Raised by German Jewish refugees, he spent the next three decades as a NYC public high school teacher, serving in the South Bronx, Harlem and Brooklyn. His play, *Roll the Dice*, co-written with Larry Kelly (AKA Miracle Larry) was performed at the NYC Theater Summerfest in September 2018. Currently, he spends his days gawking at the Manhattan skyline on his walks along the west bank of the Hudson River.

Eleni Sikelianos is a graduate of the Jack Kerouac School at Naropa, and a former curator at the Poetry Project on Second Ave. She 'came of age' as a poet at those two venues, and is the author of nine books of poetry, mostly recently *Make Yourself Happy* and *What I Knew*, and two hybrid anti-memoirs. She has received many awards for her poetry, nonfiction, and translations, and frequently collaborates with musicians, filmmakers and visual artists.

John Sinclair is an American poet, writer, and political activist from Flint, Michigan. Sinclair's defining style is jazz poetry, and he has released most of his works in audio formats, usually including musical accompaniment. He rose to prominence in the mid-1960s as manager for the radical Detroit rock band, MC5. His arrest and ten-year sentence for marijuana possession (later overturned) became a cause celebre in the 70s, including a John Lennon song for him. "From an early age I was fascinated by NYC as the center of everything interesting that was happening in America. When I started listening to jazz in 1959, I followed the exploits of great New York City musicians like Thelonious Monk, Charlie Parker and Dizzy Gillespie and then started writing about them for jazz and poetry magazines in the 1960s. I've visited NYC many times and feel extremely comfortable there."

Sean Singer is the author of *Discography* (Yale University Press, 2002), winner of the Yale Series of Younger Poets Prize, selected by W.S. Merwin, and the Norma Farber First Book Award from the Poetry Society of America; *Honey and Smoke* (Eyewear Publishing, 2015); and *Today in the Taxi* (Tupelo Press, 2022). He runs a manuscript consultation service.

Hal Sirowitz is an internationally known poet and the author of five books of poetry including the best-seller, *Mother Said* (Crown/ Random House 1996), which has been translated into thirteen languages. Sirowitz first began to attract attention at the Nuyorican Poets Café where he was a frequent competitor in their Friday night poetry Slam in the 1990's, and later appeared on MTV's *Spoken Word Unplugged*; *Lollapalooza*; Edinburgh's Fringe Festival, and other places. His poem "I Finally Managed to Speak to Her" appeared on New York City subways and buses as part of the *Poetry in Motion* series. Hal was awarded a National Endowment for the

Arts Fellowship and became the second Poet Laureate of Queens, New York, a position he held for three years.

Dr. Rommi Smith is inaugural Poet-in-Residence for British Parliament, Inaugural-Writer-in-Residence for Keats House and a three-time Writer in Residence for the BBC. A Cave Canem fellow, Rommi is also winner of the Northern Writers' Award for Poetry (selected by the poet Don Paterson). She is a recipient of a Hedgebrook Fellowship and The Elizabeth George Award. She is a Sphinx30 playwright: one of just thirty British women playwrights mentored by legendary theatre company – Sphinx Theatre. Rommi is Writer-In-Residence for TopFoto and Poet-in-Residence for the Wordsworth Trust. A Visiting Scholar at City University New York (CUNY), she has presented her work at institutions including: The Segal Theater, The Schomburg Center for Research in Black culture and City College, New York.

Gerd Stern was born on the German/French border in 1928, emigrated to the United States with his family as the Nazis rose to power, settled and grew up in Washington Heights in NYC. After a lifetime of wide travels and accomplishments, particularly in the San Francisco Bay Area, he returned to New York, where he lives in Chelsea. His life as a poet, artist, and multimedia pioneer spans 40s bohemia, 50s Beat culture, 60s hippiedom, 70s hip capitalism and beyond. His solo and collaborative multi-media projects have been exhibited at the Museum of Modern Art, Whitney Museum of American Art, Guggenheim Museum, Tate Museum, Vienna's Kunsthalle, and Centre Georges Pompidou. His oral history, *From Beat Scene Poet to Psychedelic Multimedia Artist: 1948–1978*, was published by The Bancroft Library, University of California, Berkeley.

Garland Thompson Jr. Poet, actor, playwright, producer, filmmaker, model, stage designer, former stagehand, and an occasional teacher born to a father whose life was dedicated to the Theatre. He grew up in the Theatre, first on one coast (west), then the other (east), surrounded by mad, creative people from photographers, filmmakers, and poets to actors, playwrights, painters, sculptors, writers, musicians and composers. In addition to writing, acting, teaching and making movies, he co-founded the Rubber Chicken Open Mic and Poetry Slam 14 years ago, which he still hosts at East Village Coffee Lounge in Monterey, CA. Every month or so he travels back to Brooklyn where in 2014 he took over running his father's Frank Silvera Writers Workshop, which he started with actor and producer Morgan Freeman in 1973.

Christine Timm is a native New Yorker with roots in working class Queens. She has her Ph.D. in English from City University of New York, where she studied with Allen Ginsberg and other cool cats. Along with George Guida and Bob Timm, she cohosted the initial NYC College Poetry Slams at the Bowery Poetry Club. She now cohosts the College Slam and Word events with Nick Powers at The Nuyorican Poets Café. As a stage poet, percussionist, and dancer, she's interested in play of word, body, and beat. She is an English professor at a State University of New York College.

Vincent Toro is the author of *Tertulia* (Penguin Random House, 2020) and *Stereo Island Mosaic*, which won the Poetry Society of America's Norma Farber First Book award. He is a recipient of poetry fellowships from the New York Foundation for the Arts, the New Jersey Council on the Arts, and the Poets House. Vincent is a Professor of English at Rider University, contributing editor at Kweli Literary Journal, and a Dodge Foundation poet. He dreams of a day when New York will resurrect Tramps, Twilo, and Kim's Video.

Edwin Torres is a New York City native, from the hallowed grounds of 168th Street and Grand Concourse in the Bronx. His formative adolescent poetic years were spent in the East Village, managing the Iliad of Alphabet City as a twenty-something wannabe punk, while ensconced between The Nuyorican Poets Cafe, St. Mark's Poetry Project and Dixon Place. A self-proclaimed *lingualisualist*, rooted in the languages of sight and sound, his books of poetry include: *Quanundrum: I Will Be Your Many Angled Thing* (Roof Books), *The Animal's Perception of Earth* (Doublecross Press), *Xoeteox: the Infinite Word Object* (Wave Books), and *Ameriscopia* (University of Arizona Press). Fellowships include; The Foundation for Contemporary Art, The DIA Arts Foundation, NYFA, and The Poetry Fund. Anthologies include: *Manifold Criticism, American Poets In The 21st Century: Poetics of Social Engagement, Post-Modern American Poetry Vol.2*, and *Aloud: Voices From The Nuyorican Poets Café*.

Zev Torres, in various guises, has been roaming the streets of New York City since the mid '80's in search of the fire breathing muse. His poetry has appeared in numerous print and on-line publications including Great Weather for Media's *Escape Wheel* and *Suitcase of Chrysanthemums*, Three Rooms Press' *Maintenant 6, 12* and *15*, and in his latest collection, *Stalactites and Stalagmites*. Zev's devil-be-damned approach to the creative process is also displayed in his thrill-seeking, risk-taking spoken word performances. Since 2008, Zev has hosted Make Music New York's annual Spoken Word Extravaganza and in 2010, founded the Skewered Syntax Poetry and Pub Crawls.

Tony Towle began writing poetry in the 1960s, taking workshops with Kenneth Koch and Frank O'Hara. He has received, among other awards and prizes, fellowships from the National Endowment for the Arts, the New York State Council on the Arts, the Poets Foundation, the Ingram Merrill Foundation, and the Foundation for Contemporary Arts Grants to Artists award (2015). "Although born in Manhattan, I grew up living on the sixth floor of an apartment building just off Queens Boulevard, from which I could see the distant skyline. Rego Park was the country, compared to those phalanxes of giant buildings encountered when my mother had occasion to take me to the 'city,' or when I first got to see it on my own, commuting for the eighth grade from Queens by subway to the YMCA school on Central Park West."

Jack Tricarico is a New York City painter and poet who has been published in poetry journals and anthologies in the United States, Europe, and Mexico. "Driving a taxi for 23 years at night in New York City gave me a bare ass view of a non-stop city with its pants down that was more revealing than I ever expected it to be before I started."

Quincy Troupe is the author of 21 books, including 11 volumes of poetry. His writings have been translated into over 30 languages. He is co-author with Miles Davis of *Miles: the Autobiography*; *Earl the Pearl* with Earl Monroe and the author of *Miles and Me*, a chronicle of his friendship with Miles Davis, published by Seven Stories Press in 2018. Troupe's latest books of poems are *Seduction*, a book-length poem, *Ghost Voices*, both from TriQuarterly Books, Northwestern University Press in 2018. *Duende Poems 1966 – Now*, published by Seven Stories Press in November, 2022. Among his achievements are the Paterson Award for Sustained Literary Achievement, the Milt Kessler Poetry Award, three American Book Awards, the 2014 Gwendolyn Brooks Poetry Award and a 2014 Lifetime Achievement Award from Furious Flower. Quincy Troupe is Professor Emeritus from the University of California, San Diego. He lives in Harlem (New York) with his wife, Margaret Porter Troupe.

Leah Umansky is a teacher and poet who lives in New York City, though a Long-Islander at heart. She is the author of two full length collections, *The Barbarous Century* and *Domestic Uncertainties* among others. She has been the host and curator of The Couplet Reading Series in NYC since 2011. Her poetry and prose have appeared or are forthcoming in such places as *The Bennington Review, Thrush Poetry Journal, The New York Times, Poetry, The Academy of American Poets' Poem-A-Day, Rhino,* and *Pleiades.*

Angelo Verga has appeared in over 150 poetry publications and is widely anthologized and translated. His seventh book is *Long and Short, including The Street in Your Head* (2016). He was an owner of The Cornelia Street Café in New York City, where his literary programs (1997-2015) created a home for poets and audiences alike. "I live in Harlem, a short bike ride from the Bronx, where my heart lives."

Anne Waldman has been an active member of the "Outrider" experimental poetry community, a culture she helped create and nurture for over four decades as writer, editor, teacher, performer, magpie scholar, infra-structure curator, and cultural/political activist. Her poetry is recognized in the lineage of Whitman and Ginsberg, and in the Beat, New York School, and Black Mountain trajectories of the New American Poetry. But she has moved beyond to forge an original vatic urgency and power all her own. Author of more than 50 books, including *Fast Speaking Woman, The Iovis Trilogy, Marriage: A Sentence, Manatee/Humanity* and *Trickster Feminism,* Waldman was a founder and director of the Poetry Project at St. Mark's Church in-the-Bowery and co-founded, with Allen Ginsberg, the Jack Kerouac School of Disembodied Poetics at Naropa University. She has been a fellow at the Rockefeller Foundation's Bellagio Center and at the Civitella Ranieri Foundation in Umbria; has held the Emily Harvey residency in Venice; was active in Occupy Art, an offshoot of Occupy Wall Street in New York City; and is a recipient of a 2013 Guggenheim Fellowship and the Poetry Society of America's Shelley Memorial Award, and is a Chancellor Emeritus of The Academy of American Poets. She divides her time between New York City and Boulder, Colorado and works with the Rhizoma community in Mexico City.

George Wallace is a third generation New Yorker (Brooklyn, Harlem, Long Island) who returned to NYC in 1988 after 20 years living and working abroad to create his home base for all things poetic. He is Writer in Residence at the Walt Whitman Birthplace, author of 38 chapbooks, co-editor of Great Weather for Media, and editor of this anthology. He has performed at such legendary and landmark NYC venues as Nuyorican Café, Yippie Café, Sidewalk Café, Le Poisson Rouge, Tribes Gallery, Bowery Poetry Club, Smalls Jazz Club, Manitobas, Poet's House, C-Note, Lincoln Center and Carnegie Hall. He has collaborated with David Amram, Donovan, Grant Hart, Levon Helm, Peter Max, Maddy Prior and Thurston Moore. A student of WD Snodgrass (BA, Syracuse University), Marvin Bell and David St John (MFA, Pacific University), he is adjunct professor of English at Pace University in Manhattan.

Carl Watson is a poet and fiction writer, living in New York City. His latest novel, *Only Descend,* (Autonomedia) is set in Manhattan in the late 90s. He has written for the *Village Voice, NY Press, The Williamsburg Observer, Sensitive Skin, The Brooklyn Rail, Evergreen Review, Degraphe, La Liberation* and others. Watson received the Kathy Acker Award for Fiction in 2012.

Bruce Weber is a poet and art historian who grew up in Brooklyn and Rockaway in Queens. He attended Brooklyn College and the CUNY Graduate Center. He studied poetry with Ron Padgett through the 92Y Poetry Center, and for over twenty years organized the Alternative New Year's Day Spoken Word/Performance Extravaganza in downtown Manhattan.

Joe Weil is a former tool grinder on the night shift and now an associate professor of English at Binghamton University. He has published poems, essays, reviews and stories in many journals including the *Boston Review, Paterson Literary Review, Rattle, North American Review, Ragazine, the Chicago Quarterly* and *Poet Lore.* Weil's latest book by New York Quarterly, *The Backwards Years*, appeared in August of 2020.

Francine Witte is a native New Yorker who has seen many iterations of this beautiful city. The fun teeny-bopper pseudo-hippie sixties, the gritty 70's where she temped her way around Manhattan, to now, city that just won't take it lying down, much less lie down in the first place. She is a former NYC public school teacher, and lives on the Upper East Side, where she writes poetry and flash fiction. Her books include: *Dressed All Wrong for This* (Blue Light Press,) *The Way of the Wind* (Adhoc Press,) and *Café Crazy* (Kelsay Books).

Michelle Whittaker is a NYFA Poetry Fellow and the author of *Surge* (Great Weather for MEDIA), which was awarded a 2018 Next Generation Indie Book Award. "My favorite recreation is spending several hours a day writing in my beloved Queen's Room Café in Astoria."

Jeffrey Cyphers Wright is a post-surrealist, New Romantic poet, sonneteer and author of 17 books of verse, including *Blue Lyre* (Dos Madres Press), *Fake Lies* (Fell Swoop), and *Party Everywhere* (Xanadu). Currently he publishes *Live Mag!*, a journal of art and poetry. "I'm a critic, eco-activist, impresario, filmmaker, singer/songwriter, and artist. And I like to cook and garden in my beloved East Village." He was a board member and workshop leader at the Poetry Project at St. Mark's Church and regularly hosts events at New York venues like La Mama, Howl! Happening, and the New York Public Library at Tompkins Square. He received an MFA in poetry after studying with Allen Ginsberg.

Emanuel Xavier, Latinx poet and LGBTQ activist, was born in Brooklyn, New York, and became involved in the House/ball scene as a homeless gay teen. Xavier received a New York City Council Citation for his many cultural contributions to city arts and has also been recipient of an International Latino Book Award, Lambda Literary Award nominations and American Library Association Over the Rainbow Books selections for his collections which include: *Pier Queen, Americano, If Jesus Were Gay, Nefarious, Radiance* and *Selected Poems of Emanuel Xavier.*

Anton Yakovlev is author of *Chronos Dines Alone* (SurVision Books, 2018), winner of the James Tate Prize; translator of a book of work by Sergei Yesenin. His poems have appeared in *The New Yorker,* Great Weather for Media anthologies, *KGB Bar Online Literary Review, The Long Islander, Posit,* and elsewhere. Until early 2020, Anton Yakovlev organized the weekly workshop program and curated the Triangle Quarterly reading series at Bowery Poetry Club, also co-hosting the Carmine Street Metrics reading series at Otto's Shrunken Head in Manhattan. Lately, while staying active on Zoom, he has been compensating for the lack of in-person poetry community involvement by doing the exact opposite and spending many hours hiking the more obscure mountainous trails of New York and New Jersey.

John Yau moved to New York in 1975, so he could go to the Museum of Modern Art, The Metropolitan Museum of Art, and all the other museums the city and its boroughs had to offer. His first chapbook was titled *Crossing Canal Street* (1976). Since then, he has published many books of poetry, fiction, and criticism, along with monographs and catalogues. A noted art critic and, since 2004, arts editor for *Brooklyn Rail*, Yau has also published many works of art criticism and artists' books, including *The United States of Jasper Johns* (1996). In 2020, he reviewed Lawrence Ferlinghetti's first solo exhibition of paintings in New York when he was 101. "Despite all the changes that have taken place in NYC, I still take yellow cabs and ride public transportation."

Don Yorty was born in Lebanon, Pa in 1949 and lives in NYC. A writer and garden activist, he has three published collections of poetry: *A Few Swimmers Appear*, *Poet Laundromat* (Philadelphia Eye and Ear), and *Spring Sonnets* (Indolent Books). He was included in *Out of This World, An Anthology of the Poetry of the St. Mark's Poetry Project, 1966-1991* (Crown). His novel, *What Night Forgets* (Herodias Press), was published in 2000. Recent work has been in *The Brooklyn Rail, Boog City, and Live Mag!* "Presently, I'm writing about the fight to save and preserve community gardens in NYC, a struggle that began in the 80s and continues to this day."

Bill Zavatsky recently celebrated fifty-plus years as a New Yorker, having come to the city from Connecticut, where he was born and raised, to study at Columbia University. There he earned a B.A. and later an M.F.A. from the Writing Program. He edited and published *Sun Magazine* from the early seventies and in 1975 started publishing books under the Sun imprint, nearly forty of them. He has translated Valery Larbaud, André Breton, and Robert Desnos, and has taught widely, most recently a poetry workshop in Manhattan now in its eighth year. The most recent collection of his own poetry is *Where X Marks the Spot*.

Steve Zeitlin is a folklorist, writer and cultural activist. He is the founding director of City Lore, New York City's center for urban folk culture. Described as "wise renegades," City Lore encompasses a Lower East Side gallery space, performances, lectures, the People's Hall of Fame, and POEMobile that projects poems onto walls and buildings, and programs throughout the five boroughs in tandem with live readings. He is also the co-founder of the brevitas poetry collective, including more than 60 poets who exchange work online twice a month and host an annual festival. He is the author of a volume of poetry, *I Hear America Singing in the Rain*, and his latest book is *The Poetry of Everyday Life: Storytelling and the Art of Awareness*, published by Cornell University Press.

Acknowledgments and Permissions

Grateful acknowledgement to previous publishers of work which appears in this anthology from the following poets:

Carlo Aguasaco, "From the Center of the Subway Car" (*The New York City Subway Poems*, Ashland Poetry Press, 2000);

Carol Alexander, "Amoeba, My City," (*Environments*, Dos Madres Press, 2018);

Hala Alyan, "Moral Inventory" (*Twenty Ninth Year*, Mariners Books, 2019);

Austin Alexis, "At Columbus Circle" (Tamarind Magazine);

Miguel Algarín, "Sublime" (*Survival/Supervivencia* Arte Público Press, 2009);

Dorothy Friedman August, "On the Heart of the City and How They Are Disconnected" (And Then Magazine);

Peter Balakian, "Warhol / Race Riot / 63" (Ziggurat, University of Chicago Press, 2010);

Ellen Bass, "Lightning Streak of White" (Plume);

Charles Bernstein, "The Alphabet of the Tracks" (*Topsy Turvy*, University of Chicago Press, 2021);

Anselm Berrigan, "Poem Inspired by Everything" (Can We Have Our Ball Back Magazine);

Luciann Two Feathers Berrios, "Captive" (*Words from my Collarbone: a Rebirth*, Lucian Berrios, 2021);

Max Blagg, "Second Avenue" (*Pink Instrument*, Lumen Press, 1998);

Jennifer Blowdryer, "Hell's Kitchen" (Never Apologize, Never Explain Blog);

Robert Bly, "Winter Afternoon in Greenwich Village" (*Eating Honey: New and Selected Poems*, HarperCollins, 1999);

Regie Cabico, "It's Not so Much His Kiss I Recall as His Voice" (Beltway Poetry Quarterly);

Steve Cannon, "Orange" (*ALOUD! Voices from the Nuyorican Poets Cafe*, Holt, 1994);

Melissa Castillo, "The Lovers of the Poor" (*Caticlue Eats the Apple*, Verse Seven Pulse, 2016);

Andre Codrescu, "The City" (Live Mag!);

Brenda Coultas, "In Search of Giants" (Booglit);

Steve Dalachinsky, "Subway Systems" (originally appeared in *Night in the Naked City*, NeuroNautic Press, 2019);

Toi Derricotte, "In an Urban School" (*Captivity*, University of Pittsburgh Press,1989);

JP DiBlasi, "Love on the N Train" (*No Longer Gravity's Partner*, Blue Light Press, 2019);

Diane di Prima, "Hot Plate Cooking 1955" (*Dinners and Nightmares*, Corinth Books 1961);

Margarita Drago, "New York" (*Hijas de los Vuelos*, El Mon Armado Edicions, Buenos Aires);

Denise Duhamel, "Fear on 11th and Avenue A, New York City" (*Queen For A Day: Selected and New Poems*, University of Pittsburgh Press, 2001);

Cornelius Eady, "The Ballet Called John the Baptist" (*Victims of the Latest Dance Craze*, Ommation Press, 1986);

David M. Elsasser, "Back to Futurama" (*Delicious*, NoNet Press, 2014);

Elaine Equi, "Mulberry Street" (*Decoy*, Coffee House Press, 2014), "The Courtyard", "Muffins of Sunsets" (*Sentence and Rain*, Coffee House Press 2015);

Martín Espada, "The Stoplight at the Corner Where Somebody Had to Die" (*Floaters*, WW Norton 2021);

Lawrence Ferlinghetti, "The pennycandystore beyond the El" from *A CONEY ISLAND OF THE MIND*, copyright ©1958 by Lawrence Ferlinghetti. Reprinted by permission of New Directions Publishing Corp.;

Edward Field, "Statue of Liberty" (*After the Fall*, University of Pittsburgh Press 2007);

Karen Finneyfrock, "Newer Colossus" (*We Will Be Shelter: Poems for Survival*, Write Bloody Press, 2010);

Stewart Florsheim, "Elevator to the A Train" (*A Split Second of Light*, Blue Light Press, 2011);

Diane Frank, "Venantius" (*While Listening to the Enigma Variations*, Glass Lyre Press, 2021);

Philip Fried, "The Quantum Mechanics of Everyday Life" (Agni Magazine, Verse Daily) (*Squaring the Circle*, Salmon Poetry, 2017);

Frank X. Gaspar, "Late Rapturous" (The Tampa Times);

Phillip Giambri, "A Broken Bed and Bodega Beer" (*The Amorous Adventures of Blondie and Boho*, 2020);

Tony Gloeggler, "Mid Life Poetry Crises" (New York Quarterly);

Philip Good, "Lewis Warsh" (*Poets in a Box or Pluto in Motion*, Reality Beach, 2018);

George Guida, "The Good People of New York City" (Italian American Writers Blog);

Nathalie Handal, "Takes on the Bowery" (*Life in a Country Album*, University of Pittsburgh Press, 2019);

Robert Hershon, "Rick's Liquors" (*Blue Shovel*, Hanging Loose Press, 1978);

Edward Hirsch, "Eight People" (*Together in a Strangeness: America's poets Respond to the Pandemic*, Knopf, 2020);

Jack Hirschman, "Balaban" (first appeared in *Black Alephs*, Trigram Press, London 1969, and was reprinted in *Front Lines*, City Lights Books 2002);

Roxanne Hoffman, "Flora Selva" (*The Riverside Poetry Workshop Poems*, Vol. 8, 2004);

Bob Holman, "A Real Life Stage and Like a Punk Festival and a Cool and Loud Salsa" (*The Unspoken*, Bowery Books, 2019);

Marie Howe, "After the Movie" (*Kingdom of Ordinary Time*, WW Norton, 2008);

Matthew Hupert, "Outside Ottomanelli's" (appeared originally in *Ism is a RetroVirus*, Three Rooms Press, 2011);

Hettie Jones, "For Margaret of Sixth Street" (*Doing 70*, Hanging Loose, 2007);

Jennifer Juneau, "A Kind of Love" (*Sensitive Skin Writing*, Home Planet News);

David Lehman, "World Trade Center" (*Valentine Place*, Scribner, 1996);

Jean Lehrman, Just War (*Lazarus*, Rogue Scholar Press, 2007);

Linda Lerner, "Times Square: the Crossroads" (Misfit Magazine, *Taking the F train*, NYQ 2021);

M.L. Liebler, "The Jazz" (*Written in the Rain: New and Selected Poems*, Tiebot Bach, 2000);

Maria Lisella, "Queens Classics" (Queens Poets);

Ellaraine Lockie, "Survival Guide" (Ibbetson Street)

Paul Mariani, "The Republic" (*The Great Wheel: Poems*, Norton, 1996);

Julio Marzán, "Subway Stairs at Spring Street" (Prairie Schooner);

Mindy Matijasevic, "With Women and Children on the Street" (Home Planet News);

Bernadette Mayer, "Key Foods" (*Another Smashed Pinecone*, United Artists Publishers, 1998);

Jesús Papoleto Meléndez, "Fair for Fare" (*Papolitico – Poems from a Political Persuasion*, 2 Leaf Editions, 2018);

Nancy Mercado, *Rooms for the Living: New York Poems*, 2004, Binghamton University, Doctoral degree;

Sharon Mesmer, "Lou Reed's New York" (Hanging Loose);

Frank Murphy, "When Our Ancestors Ate Each Other, and They Did" (Home Planet News);

David Mills, "Talking to the Teeth" (*Boneyarn*, Ashland University Press 2021);

Eileen Myles, "A Poem" (*I Must Be Living Twice/new and selected poems*, HarperCollins, 2015);

Charles North, "Something" (Study for "Everything," *Everything and Other Poems*, Song Cave, 2020);

D Nurkse, "Letter from Brooklyn" (Manhattan Review);

Obsidian, "A Train Away" (Zen is Now);

Alicia Ostriker, "Crosstown" (*No Heaven*, 2005, reprinted by permission of Univ of Pittsburgh Press);

Yuko Otomo, "Two Poems" (*Study and Other Poems on Art*, Ugly Duckling Press, 2013);

Ron Padgett, "Dog" (*Collected Poems*, Coffee House Press, 2013);

Puma Perl, "Past and Pandemic" (Chelsea Community News);

Simon Pettet, "Poem" (*After Mayakovsky*) (*Hearth*, Talisman Books, 2008);

Meg Pokrass, "Before the Audition: Times Square 1990" (prose version in *Spinning to Mars*, Blue Light Press, 2020);

Juana M. Ramos, "New York City – Part Two" (*Sin Ambages/ To the Point*, Colombia, 2020);

Thaddeus Rutkowski, "In the Tunnel" (Poetry Pacific), (Border Crossings Sensitive Skin Press, 2018);

Nicole Santalucia, "The Cannoli Machine at the Brooklyn Detention Center" (*Because I Did Not Die*, Bordighera Press, 2015);

Robert Scotellaro, "Caruso Sweating & Big Nick in His Underwear" (Vagabond);

Christopher Seid, "Leaving New York City" (*Age of Exploration*, Blue Light Press, 2015);

Alan Semerdjian, "Evening in Gravesend" (Xanadu);

Vijay Seshadri, "Immediate City" (*The Long Meadow*, Graywolf Press, 2003);

Eleni Sikelianos, "The Monster Lives of Boys and Girls" (*The Monster Lives of Boys and Girls*, Green Integer Press, 2003);

John Sinclair, "round about midnight" (*always know: a book about monk, vol 1 & 2*, Trembling Pillow Press, 2020);

Sean Singer, "Schism" (*Two Horatio*, Tupelo Press, 2022);

Rommi Smith, "Alice: Prospect Park, Springtime" (written with the assistance of a Northern Writers' Award from New Writing North);

Gerd Stern, "fr The Apple" (*New Yorker Kunst Gechichten*, Kat Schuetz Verlag fur modern Kunst Nurnberg, 2011);

Garland Thompson Jr., "Blow Bad Blues Brother Lateef" (Polarity, 2006);

Christine Timm, "Sleeping with Gregory Corso" (Smalls Books, 2010);

Edwin Torres, "No YoYo" (*Quanundrum*, Roof Books 2021);

Tony Towle, "Municipal Cartography" (*History of the Invitation: New and Selected Poems 1963-2000*, Hanging Loose Press, 2008);

Jack Tricarico, "In the Fisted Hand of May" (Hunger Magazine);

Quincy Troupe, "The Day Duke Raised: May 24 1984" (*Snake-Back Solos*, I Reed Books division of Reed & Cannon, 1978) *Transcircularities*, (Coffee House Press, 2015), *Duende: Poems, 1966-Now* (Seven Stories Press, New York, 2022);

Anne Waldman, "Show You Out the Door" (*Outrider*, La Alameda Press 2006);

George Wallace, "Walking on Tenth Street" (*Poppin' Johnny*, Three Rooms Press, 2008);

Carl Watson, "125th Street" (Sensitive Skin, 2018);

Bruce Weber, "my sister magdalena was engaged to be married to giuseppe" (Poetry Justice);

Jeffrey Cyphers Wright, "Classic Madhatten" (Hanging Loose Magazine);

Emanuel Xavier, "Bushwick Bohemia" (*Selected Poems of Emanuel Xavier*, Rebel Satori Press, 2021);

Anton Yakovlev, "First Snow" (*Neptune Court*, The Operating System, 2015);

Bill Zavatsky, "104 Bus Uptown" (*Where X Marks The Spot*, 2000, Hanging Loose Press, 2006).

Thanks to Jeff Wright, Nancy Mercado and Bob Holman for their curatorial assistance in suggesting poets for this anthology; to Francine Witte, for her co-production assistance; and to Valery Oisteanu, for his cover photo, and to Steve Dalachinsky for his painting illustrations, and BA Van Sise, for his photo which prompted Jane Hirshfield's poem.

"Liberty or Death" by Steve Dalachinsky

CPSIA information can be obtained
at www.ICGtesting.com
Printed in the USA
BVHW030947070322
630812BV00002B/27

9 781421 837178